WINTER IN JULY

Visits with Children's Authors Down Under

by
JANET CRANE BARLEY

The Scarecrow Press, Inc.
Metuchen, N.J., & London
1995

Top of the News. June 1974, 30, 373-393. By Ivan Southall. "Real Adventure Belongs to Us." Reprinted with permission of the Association for Library Service to Children and the Young Adult Library Services Association, Divisions of the American Library Association (50 E. Huron St., Chicago, IL 60611). From *Top of the News,* 1974, Copyright © 1974.

Reprinted with the permission of Macmillan Publishing Company, a division of Macmillan, Inc. from *A Journey of Discovery* by Ivan Southall. Copyright © 1975 Ivan Southall.

British Library Cataloguing-in-Publication data available

Library of Congress Cataloging-in-Publication Data

Barley, Janet Crane, 1934-
  Winter in July: visits with children's authors down under / by Janet Crane Barley
    p. cm.
  Includes bibliographical references.
  ISBN 0-8108-2945-2 (acid-free paper)
  1. Children's literature, Australian—History and criticism— Theory, etc. 2. Children's literature, New Zealand—History and criticism—Theory, etc. 3. Authors, Australian—20th century— Interviews. 4. Authors, New Zealand—20th century—Interviews. 5. Children's literature—Authorship. I. Title.
  PR9613.9.B37 1995
  820.9'9282'0994—dc20   94-33216

To my husband, Morry, who insisted I take the trip when I didn't think it was practical.

And to Mary Lou White who created the adventures that led to this book.

CONTENTS

ACKNOWLEDGEMENTS

I have many people to thank for their part in this book. I am grateful beyond measure to the authors who gave these presentations and took time from their own creative projects to graciously edit my transcripts.

I also thank librarians from Dayton-Montgomery County and Washington Township systems, Dot Bickley for providing extensive background information, Pat Glossip for proofreading, Joe Reuwer and Liz Taylor for technical support, Bev Runkle for her trip videos, and Sandra Barley, Bob Bone, Diane Cormac, Lillian Dinos, Nan Kienow, Susie Kircher, Jane Munster, Bob Steffes, Dorothy Wagner, Dorothy Waterfill, and Edith Whittaker for their special contributions.

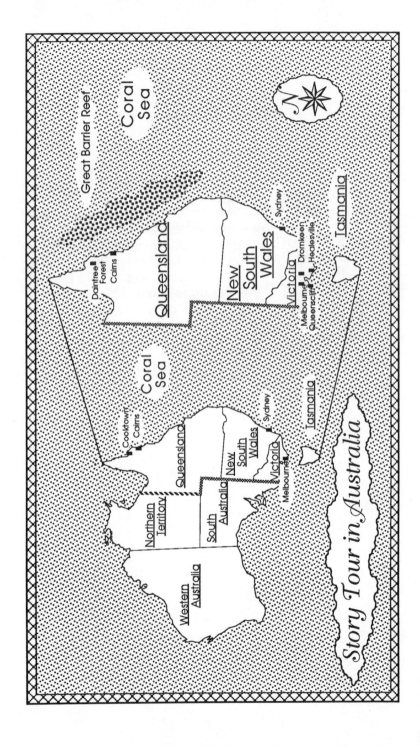

Story Tour in Australia

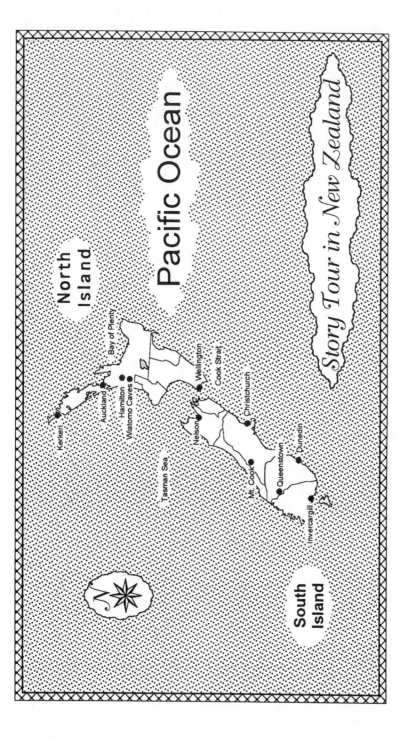

INTRODUCTION

This is actually three books in one. You will read what some leading New Zealand and Australian children's authors say about their books and children's literature in their countries. You'll learn techniques of successful writers. And you'll gain perspective on life "Down Under."

I visited these authors on a Literature Down Under story tour with a group of 42 librarians, teachers, readers, and writers led by Dr. Mary Lou White, a retired professor of children's literature who chaired the Caldecott Awards committee in 1992.

Literature Down Under was my second story tour. On a 1990 story tour to England, not only did we explore London, stay in a dorm in Cambridge, and follow the path of the Canterbury pilgrims, but we met some of the most fascinating British children's writers. Before we went to Helen Cresswell's house, I was introduced to a ghost at Belton Hall, the place that inspired her book *Moondial.* After we had lunch at Phillipa Pearce's house, we saw that Tom's midnight garden was still intact. Kevin Crossley-Holland read to us from his folktales while we sat beside the North Sea pool where a seal-woman taught him to swim. What a book that trip would have made!

When I heard there would be a story tour to New Zealand and Australia, I was sure the authors' presentations would make an equally good book about children's books, imagination and creativity. I didn't anticipate how much we would learn from them about the different view from the other side of the world.

A large map I saw at a newsstand in Kuranda, a village in Australia's rain forest, is a metaphor that stays with me. Australia and the rest of the Southern Hemisphere are at the top of the map. North America, with Florida's finger pointing northward, is near the bottom. It reminds me that things may look different from different directions and that concepts I accept as inviolate might not be.

Before I started research for the trip, I lumped the two countries in one mental package. Early on I was cautioned that there were many differences and I would offend people by sticking Australia and New Zealand together as if they were two states under a single flag. Since the United States has that common bond of starting as a British colony with Australia and New Zealand, I was interested to compare how each evolved with such distinct personalities, even though the British tried to create another England wherever they settled.

Christchurch, New Zealand, is called "the most English city outside of England." Some buildings were duplicated so faithfully to British plans that those which face south to catch the winter sunlight in the Northern Hemisphere also face south in the Southern Hemisphere—away from the valued winter sun. When you stand in the quadrangle of the neo-Gothic gray stone Arts Centre of Christchurch, the former campus of Canterbury University, you could just as well be on a British campus. But walk down toward Canterbury Park and the Avon River, and the landscape is distinctly New Zealand.

Drawings of early Australian homesteads look just like Old England with oak trees and other typical English greenery. But experts say those trees probably hadn't yet taken root in foreign soil. Settlers, who commissioned those drawings to send home to show friends and relatives how successful they were, asked artists to set their homes in an English landscape. They were sure no one would be impressed unless the landscape looked like "home."

As soon as the settlers could, they chopped down unique native gum trees and scrub and replaced them with deciduous trees from the Northern Hemisphere. Now people value the native vegetation and are somewhat disdainful of "introduced" plants and animals.

Both countries have an indigenous population maltreated almost out of existence by settlers and now they are looking to their ancient wisdoms for modern truths.

Gavin Bishop, New Zealand illustrator and author, told us a little about Maori history and folklore. He mentioned how missionaries built mission schools in New Zealand where they strove to stamp out Maori culture and make all the Maori children into pseudo-Europeans who could name all the tributaries of the Danube. I realized then that there were more methods to kill a way of life than the wars American settlers waged on Indians.

Mark MacLeod, children's publishing director of Random House Australia, described how Aboriginal traditions are influencing children's literature, and some of the controversy surrounding these books. After we discovered that in 40,000 years of living in Australia, Aborigines never needed a word for time, we talked about a world without time and clocks and deadlines and decided that was almost beyond our imagining.

Children's literature in Australia and New Zealand is a rather new phenomenon which has come into its own within the past decade or so. The dearth of books set in their own countries was a simple matter of economics. New Zealand's population is just under 3.5 million—about the same as the city of Los Angeles or the state of Kentucky. Australia has one million fewer people than the state of New York.

For many years, publishers assumed there weren't enough people in New Zealand or Australia to support publication of their own children's literature, and that the rest of the world was not clamoring for books set somewhere south of the equator. Children in the Southern Hemisphere grew up reading books published in Great Britain which were rich in British details like snowy Christmases, a totally foreign tradition to Australians and New Zealanders. They celebrate their hot summer Christmases with a barbecue or a day at the beach.

Some authors described their imaginative dislocation because British books were the only ones available to them. Margaret Mahy told us that the influences of British books gave children in New Zealand a clear impression that their world was not important—only things British mattered. Now her grandchildren can choose books reflecting their homeland.

Often Australia and New Zealand are stereotyped as nations of sports and horses. Less well known is their extraordinarily high literacy rate. New Zealand has the highest literacy rate in the world with Australia's following closely. Mark MacLeod characterizes Australians as "great book buyers."

We could see the evidence for ourselves as we visited busy, well-stocked bookstores in both countries. In Sydney at the Children's Book Fair, one event of Children's Book Week, we were impressed with the number of children eagerly buying books and leaving with bags bulging with their purchases.

Publishers may have underestimated the worldwide market in books by children's authors from Australia and New Zealand. According to Mr. MacLeod, Graeme Base's *Animalia* sold over 250,000 copies and Mem Fox's *Possum Magic* sold 500,000 copies worldwide. Mr. MacLeod said he'd be surprised if many Australian authors of adult literature have sold such large numbers of books internationally.

He mentioned that the growth areas in Australian publishing are children's and self-help books and that 27 to 30 percent of all titles published in Australia are children's books. He publishes 18 to 20 children's titles per year.

In 10 years the New Zealand children's literature industry has gone from nothing to being a bigger export earner than the fine New Zealand wines, according to Betty Gilderdale, professor and scholar of children's literature.

Even so, Gavin Bishop says 3,000 copies is considered about the number a good children's book can expect to sell there, although some do sell more.

Co-publishing, with publishers from two or more countries getting together to produce a book, is a common way to extend the print run (and profitability of a book). But British and American publishers tend to avoid books with a strong New Zealand or Australian flavor.

Walter McVitty, who currently publishes children's books under the Walter McVitty imprint, explains that special quality: "From Australian children's books one can sense the somewhat mystical power that the land itself exerts on its creative writers, painters, and composers who seem compelled to use their land, and their response to it, as a major theme in their work. Whereas a particular background and setting might be almost incidental in American or British writing, it is almost crucial here."

Some of the authors profiled here discussed whether books written in Australia and New Zealand should be generic with language and settings that could be anywhere in the world, or specific, conveying landscapes, conditions, and viewpoints that are unique to their area. Publishers in other countries are more likely to co-publish generic books.

Gavin Bishop says, "I think publishers are more conservative than their readers. I know that in New Zealand we have always been delighted to get a book with the strong flavor of a country. I think it's sad we're being expected to homogenize with books that could go anywhere and fit anything. A special quality is lost in a book that could be set anyplace."

Language is a common tussle between writers and publishers. Australian author Robin Klein remarks on the number of reviews she has read that say something like, "This book is good, but American children might have trouble coping with the Australianisms."

Mrs. Klein calls that attitude "rubbish" and asserts that those people are underestimating the intelligence of children. "Kids can cope with a lot more than we give them credit for. I think by changing words into your own idiom, you're denying them a chance to learn other terminology. Australian kids cope quite well with American terms that aren't common here, like 'homeroom.' Now all kids know what an 'anorak' is from reading English books. Kids read it and they get the sense of it."

To prepare for the trip, I read more than four dozen books, many by the authors we met. I'm convinced that books with a strong sense of another place provide a rich and valuable reading experience for children and adults. I would like to see these books published in the United States with the story, setting, flavor, and vocabulary unchanged. But I would add a glossary to define some unfamiliar terms for American readers. I was unsure what "plonk," "swot" and "stroppy" meant, and I was glad to find translations in the British dictionary from my bookshelf. My guesses weren't always on the mark.

When writers talk about their writing, I'm eager to listen. I want to know about the nucleus of truth that evolves into a book. Did an incident, a place, or a person inspire the plot?

Was it from firsthand experience, from observations, or from newspaper clippings? These authors told us so much more.

As the writers described the way they wrote, I learned about both the individuality and universality of the creative process. I found it reassuring to hear Robin Klein admit to being a messy writer—to learn that her marvelous prose comes not directly from some clever muse, but through a process of lists prepared and crossed out and pages done, redone, and done yet again.

I was intrigued with the way Tessa Duder creates her characters and plots her stories. I was impressed when Ivan Southall told of how his carefully plotted *Hills End* story took on a life of its own as he wrote it. I was consoled when Gavin Bishop confessed he tended to procrastinate before getting immersed in a project. I was fascinated as Peter Gouldthorpe described the layers of meaning an artist could add to a simple story. I was inspired to strive for greater originality when John Marsden described his techniques for avoiding clichés and stale writing.

As I listened to each author, I thought of Dorothy Butler's story of how her granddaughter's story strikes a real blow for books and that a love of books is one of the most valuable gifts we can give any child.

In addition to meeting with authors in their homes or other places off the typical tourist path, we had many other opportunities to learn about children's books. We heard presentations from staff at the National Library of New Zealand in Auckland and the Library of New South Wales in Sydney. Each has a comprehensive range of books for children and young people.

At Dromkeen, which houses *the* outstanding collection of historical and contemporary children's literature of Australia and also is a repository for primary reference material, staff showed us treasures from the archives.

One Monday morning a few of us watched a teacher coach one small enthusiastic girl in the Reading Recovery program at an Auckland school, and we heard about the methods that influence New Zealand's remarkably high literacy rate.

A highlight of the trip, which ranked right up there with the trip to the Great Barrier Reef, was the Australian Children's Book of the Year Awards Presentation at the Sydney Town Hall. We were delighted to see Jeannie Baker win just two days after we visited with her. Following the awards, we joined authors, publishers, and others for an elegant lunch in the Northern Foyer of the Sydney Opera House overlooking Sydney Harbour.

During the trip, I recorded all of the presentations on audiotape. After I got home, I transcribed the scratchy tapes with some difficulty and some odd results. Since these were informal remarks, sometimes interrupted with a question, I did a little gentle editing and reorganizing. Then I sent them off to the writers for review.

Several authors asked that I emphasize to all who read this book that the chapters are based on the spoken word. Although writing down what was said conveys a sense of intimacy and the chatty feel of a casual visit, it totally fails to capture the authors' skillful writing styles.

After learning about the authors, I'm sure you'll want to read some of their books and experience their writings firsthand. Many of the authors' books have been published in U.S. editions and are accessible here. Books published overseas may not be readily available, so I've included information for ordering such books.

I debated about which spelling and grammar styles to use. At first I thought it would add color to the pieces to use "colour" and "flavour" and other bits of British-based spellings, as the authors do. I decided that generally I'd follow American styles because it would be easier for me and my spell checker to be consistent. For specific terms, as in a book title or place name, like "Playcentre," I've used the New Zealand or Australian spellings.

I have divided the book into a New Zealand section and an Australian section. Each section begins with an expert's overview of that country's children's literature. Chapters follow in the order the authors were met.

The project has been more complicated than I expected and as it draws to a close, I think about what Winston Churchill said: "Writing is an adventure. To begin with, it is a toy and an amusement. Then it becomes a mistress, then it becomes a master, then it becomes a tyrant. The last phase is that just as you are about to be reconciled to your servitude, you kill the monster and fling him to the public."

As I transcribed tapes and heard the talks over and over, as I got letters from the authors, as I did additional research, I've relived this trip and found the experience rich and pleasurable, for the most part. Now I look forward to flinging the monster to the public. I hope you will enjoy this armchair version of the Literature Down Under story tour.

BETTY GILDERDALE

Betty Gilderdale, a professor and scholar of children's literature, wrote the definitive book on the history of New Zealand's children's literature, another on New Zealand children's authors, and the children's literature section of the *Oxford Companion to New Zealand Literature*. She brought a wide assortment of books for us to examine when she visited with us in a meeting room at our hotel, the White Heron, in Auckland. Her husband, who illustrates some of the children's books she writes, accompanied her.

I'm confident of the fact you must all be feeling rather jet-lagged and rather tired and I know how it is when I go to the United States or Canada. I don't know if I could sustain an evening lecture. So if any of you want to drop off, I won't take it personally.

It's nice to be with you. If you want to stop me and ask questions as I go along, please feel free to do that. We'll start off with New Zealand as we know it at the moment, that is to say a mix of European and Maori. The country actually became a colony of Britain in 1840, when the British government signed the Treaty of Waitangi with the Maori.

Ever since, one could say that there were two preoccupations in New Zealand literature. One would be the encounter with the Maori—a different race, with different habits, different customs. The second is a preoccupation with the land itself in New Zealand. Something we share with the Maori is that the land of New Zealand exerts its own influence.

As you know, we have two large islands and a smaller one. New Zealand is extremely mountainous. Even here in Auckland, where we live close to the sea, every time we go out of the house, we are climbing quite a steep hill, either up away from the sea or down to it.

Because the North Island is subtropical, the hills are covered with native bush right up to the snow line. That is

1

subtropical rain forest. I believe you've all been out to
Karekare to see Dorothy Butler today. We also have a
holiday house at Karekare. We have an acre there. The bush
is so dense once I remember I went out into the bush in the
back of our house and absolutely got lost.

It is so easy to lose yourself in New Zealand's bush.
There are no native mammals, you see. Where in the
Northern Hemisphere you have deer or foxes or squirrels to
make a little track, here we have nothing like that. Kiwis
don't make those little tracks. And so our bush is very, very
dense and very, very wild. Very rugged country.

Then, because we sit between two oceans, we have very
heavy rainfall. When you go to the South Island, you'll see
these great rivers. Of course they've had that great drought
down there, but you can see from the pebbles on the shore
how wide they would be when full.

You're warned you must never camp on the sides of the
river because if the snow melts or if there is an avalanche in
the mountains, suddenly an enormous amount of water can
come down and you can be swept off and drowned very
quickly.

And, of course, the weather is very changeable, as you
probably noticed between today and yesterday.

We once had a guest who said, "In the antipodes people
always know which way the wind is blowing." We said,
"That's right, we do. Because if it's a southerly, it's cold.
And if it's a northerly, it's warm. And if it's easterly, it
storms. And if it's westerly, that's just normal with a
procession of clouds and a bit of wind and showers and
rain." So it's changeable weather.

And then we have earthquakes. We have this major fault
line which goes through from Rotorua in the middle of the
North Island through Wellington and down through Nelson
which is at the top of the South Island.

And we've got volcanoes. Auckland is on a volcanic
plateau and Mt. Eden is a dormant volcano here. It isn't
actually extinct. And Rangitoto, the volcano which came up
in the ocean not so very long ago geologically, is only
dormant.

So you know there were a lot of things that are very,
very different. The settlers coming from the flat plains of

northern Europe had never encountered anything like this. They'd never encountered earthquakes and volcanoes and such sudden temperature changes and such floods and such rainfall.

Because the settlers in New Zealand, for the most part, didn't come until the 1860s, we're well documented. We have very good records of their diaries and letters they sent home.

The poor old early settlers complained about the weather and the difficulties of clearing the bush to make farms. And about mosquitoes and the sand flies. And the fact that it took a year to get a reply to a letter. By the time they sent a letter over, it took six months to get to England and six months to get back again. And the distances from a doctor—sometimes they lived 50 miles from a doctor. And all those things which you had in the States as well.

That immediate impact ceased after about 1914. But ever since the 1960s, there's been a bit of resurgence in books about the early settlers.

Elsie Locke, in Christchurch, is one of the authors writing on that theme. The Children's Literature Association of New Zealand gave her an award for distinguished services to New Zealand children's literature a week ago. I was a founding member of that group, which has been going about 25 years now.

Elsie Locke's book, *The Runaway Settlers,* is a New Zealand classic. It's about a woman and her children who run away from a drunken husband in Australia and come to New Zealand and to make their own way.

In another book of hers *Canoe in the Mist,* she very cleverly combined the early-settler theme and the-meeting-the-Maori theme along with a volcanic eruption. Mt. Tarawera was a beautiful volcanic mountain, which had very famous pink and white terraces. It simply blew up in 1886. Quite incredible, of course. The volcano had given a theme to Elsie Locke. Her book *Canoe in the Mist* is a story of what happened to the early settlers who were on the shore near Mt. Tarawera.

The modern books about the settlers are rather different. Earlier books were based on early diaries and letters written by a more literate and educated people. The modern books have tended to go back to the working-class people, who didn't leave as many written records. They've concentrated more, a lot more, on how hard people had to work planting, and milking and shearing and bread-making and bottling and soap-making and spinning and weaving and dressmaking and darning. There's absolutely no end to the work for the early settlers.

I think they made a virtue of necessity because much was made of the Protestant work ethic, which was brought into the country by Scottish Presbyterians. I'm sure I don't have to say much about that to a USA audience.

Now I speak as an Englishwoman and I'm telling you the work ethic doesn't hold great sway in England. Work in England is not in and of itself necessarily good.

I noticed with some interest that the work in question here is usually the sort of work that brings in money. Things like rearing children at home or painting pictures or writing books are not quite counted in the work ethic thing, because they don't make profits. The early settlers in New Zealand were certainly like that. And we will see some of the results of the work ethic I think in other directions.

Once the settlers settled, there was a golden period in New Zealand's history between the two World Wars. They had a very comfortable arrangement with Britain, because New Zealand raised sheep and farm and dairy products, which they shipped off to England and England shipped back machinery.

This was an excellent arrangement and New Zealanders felt very close to Britain and they referred to Britain as "Home." Up until the 1960s, when you heard older New Zealanders, particularly, talking about "Home," they meant Britain. Since England has gone into the common market, that has been a very different thing and attitudes toward England in New Zealand have dramatically changed.

But books about those years between the World Wars, which were very settled, were sort of sunny family novels. There were sheep stations that were well stocked. There were country events. And there were abundant food and great baking days when the tins were filled with cakes and biscuits. And the jams were sold at agricultural shows. And bottled fruit stood in serried ranks in glass jars in the larder.

Actually, when I started working on *A Sea Change,* my book which is a history of New Zealand children's literature, people all said, "Well, there isn't any New Zealand children's literature." But I discovered there had been 800 books written before 1978, starting in 1833

Before I wrote the book, I would have thought if anyone asked, "What is the national dish of New Zealand?" somebody would have said "roast lamb" or "Pavlova"— New Zealand's special meringue dessert. But no, not according to New Zealand children's literature.

According to New Zealand children's literature, the national dish would be scones. Do you have scones in the States? You know, you rub fat into flour and add egg and bake them and serve them with jam and tea. Well, scones must be the national dish, because in books they appeared for morning tea, afternoon tea, lunch, supper, even, if pushed, for breakfast. In any emergency the first thing mother did was rush into the kitchen and make scones. And everybody would be restored to cheerfulness and order.

Well, once the settlers were settled and the land was as tamed as it ever would be, the real preoccupation with the land was no longer taming it for agriculture. The preoccupation with the land expressed itself in adventure stories and, of course, New Zealand is a marvelous country for adventure.

I worked out a summary of the average adventure story. This would be a summary of New Zealand adventure stories perhaps up to about the mid-1980s. They've altered a bit since then.

Firstly, there would be twins. There is an extraordinary number of fictional twins in New Zealand. Must be something to do with twin lambs or something. Twins on a New Zealand sheep station learn that their aunt in England has been killed in a car crash and that their cousin is to come live with them.

After his arrival, they decide to introduce him to the New Zealand bush. They go suitably equipped for a tramping holiday. Unfortunately, they lose their way and narrowly escape drowning when they unwisely camp by a river. Of course, it suddenly floods after heavy rains in the mountains. They finally find shelter in a cave, where they discover Maori artifacts. But they become aware that there are other people searching for the artifacts, who want to smuggle them abroad.

The sinister intruders are South Americans. I don't know why South Americans were the villains of the piece in New Zealand adventure stories, but frequently they were.

Well, the children escape and they manage to catch the attention of a helicopter that had been sent to search for them. And once they are restored to their families, they set out to trap the smugglers, which they do with the aid of an old trapper who lives in a shack. The smugglers are brought to justice, and the children are guests of honor when the artifacts are presented to a local museum.

You would be surprised at how many New Zealand adventure stories that summary might fit. The only thing they've left out is an earthquake. Perhaps I should have put in an earthquake. Perhaps when they were in the cave or something. Earthquakes were a preoccupation of the adventure story.

The Maori artifacts, of course, bring me to the Maori components. Well, now, the earliest books were written by the missionaries and they were always sympathetic to the Maori. But land disputes arose and for some years after the Treaty of Waitangi, there were land wars between the Maori and the settlers.

Well, of course, that gave tremendous opportunity for exciting adventure stories. But those were not written by New Zealanders. There was a great craze for boys' stories at the time in the late Victorian period and people like G. A. Henty and Jules Verne made very good capital out of these fierce Maori and the wars that were going on. I think they rather did the same with the American Indians, as well.

If New Zealand writers were writing at all, they tended to stress much more that this was a terrible situation. But there was always friendship between an individual Maori and an individual white settler. And that friendship was important, even though the Maori tribe might be at war with the Europeans. That theme of friendship was a very, very constant one.

For a long time after those initial books about the land wars, people were very hesitant to raise the specter of land wars again. There were few books about them until recently. We've had books like R. L. Bacon's *Again the Bugles Blow* and Anne de Roo's *Jacky Nobody*. She wrote the story of the Maori chieftain, Hone Heke, seen through the eyes of a boy, who was part Maori, part European and felt himself to be neither one nor the other. That is why he called himself Jacky Nobody.

Interestingly, the early books were always written from the point of view of the white settlers and the Maori were the villains of the piece. Whereas these later books have been a much more balanced viewpoint really, saying what a tragic situation the land wars had been.

More recently there have been retellings of Maori legends. Ron Bacon has done some lovely retellings. His book *The House of the People* has the most beautiful illustrations by a Maori artist. The very mannered sort of illustrations actually tell the story of the Maori meeting houses. This book gives details of the customs and how they began. It was a seminal book when it came out in the 1970s.

If you do go to the Auckland War Memorial Museum, you'll see a Maori meeting house. The museum actually has the finest collection of Polynesian and Maori artifacts in the world.

The other aspect of Maori culture which has rubbed off, but I'll come back to it, is the old person. The Maori have a great respect for age and the aging person, and they also have a very extended family. The custom often was that the youngest child was given to the widowed grandmother to look after and be with her and be a companion to her. The Maori grandmother is very much a feature in many children's books.

Typical of the Maori grandmother stories is *The Kuia and the Spider,* by Patricia Grace, an award-winning book about a competition between a Maori grandmother and a spider about whose grandchildren were best.

That respect for old people and the feeling of importance of old people, along with the Maori openness about death, have become two of the most distinctive features in New Zealand children's literature. Because of that treatment of old age and of death, there are an enormous number of elderly characters in New Zealand books.

Often it is the elder characters, not the younger ones, who are very nonconformist. You remember, I mentioned a hermit in that adventure story. Those solitary men living in rabbiters *wharries* (i.e., shacks) are a regular feature in New Zealand stories. They live off the land. They value their freedom and independence much more than conventional comforts.

Instead of a literature of hippie young going off to do their thing, we have a literature of hippie old, so you might say, going off to do their own thing. And there are a lot of strong-minded old ladies who are always treated with love and respect.

I'm sure you all know about Margaret Mahy's book *Memory*. Margaret wrote that book as a result of having her own old aunt, of whom she was very fond, suffering from Alzheimer's disease. Margaret lived next door to her.

It's a wonderful book about a young man who meets up with this old lady in the middle of the night. She's pushing a trolley along in a supermarket car park. He gets worried about her and thinks he ought to take her home. Of course, when he speaks to her, she thinks he's somebody else.

When he gets her home, he realizes the awful state her house is in and he feels he ought to do something about it. It's a very clever study of her memories as a sort of counterpoint with his memories.

We never laugh *at* her, we laugh *with* her. Sometimes there are some funny episodes that her illness has led her to. But she never loses her dignity. I think Margaret achieved a perfectly accurate portrait of an old lady with Alzheimer's that still enabled her to keep her dignity. Her books are so sympathetic. Before Margaret decided to do a degree, she thought she'd like to be a nurse and she did actually work for a while in a hospital, where she spent a month or two in a geriatric ward.

Margaret Mahy was first being published in 1960, which was when we had a sort of resurgence in feeling that New Zealand books should be about New Zealand. There were a number of stories with titles like *On a Farm in New Zealand* or *Kuma is a Maori Girl*. And Margaret's stories about witches and wizards and pirates were seen as not being *New Zealand.*

She had great difficulty getting any publisher to take her books in New Zealand. She sent stories to our very good *School Journal,* which is put out into schools.

When they sent editions of the *New Zealand School Journal* into the United States, Mrs. Watts of the publishing company, Franklin Watts, saw Margaret's short stories. She decided they would make wonderful picture books.

Mrs. Watts actually launched Margaret's books in the States and in England, where they were published jointly with Dent. They knew a great deal more about her overseas, before she was known in New Zealand, because New Zealand perceived her as being not a *New Zealand* writer.

As I've been trying to say, actually when you know New Zealand, you can see Margaret is in many ways a typical New Zealand writer, particularly her preoccupation with old age and death. The witches and wizards and pirates in her books are the nonconformists of society. They are forces of energy who just turn everything around and make everyone see things in a different way. They are the catalysts of society.

In *The Haunting*, which won the Esther Glen medal for her, there's a family with a tradition of having wizards, not witches, but wizards. An old grandmother dominates the whole family—the extended family, as well.

Finally, the quiet, studious girl of the family lets it be known that, in fact, she is the family wizard. She also tells her family that the grandmother was born a magician and, when she was quite young, she did a dreadful thing with her power. That frightened her so that she set herself to crush the magic right out of her life by tidying and ordering everything too tightly. When she killed her magic, she killed other good things, including her own specialness.

The Haunting is an example of Margaret's insistence that if you over-organize, you're going to lose the sort of freedom which creativity needs.

Of course, I could spend the whole of this time with you on Margaret Mahy, but I'm concentrating today on what I see as the New Zealand aspect of her work. And I have to tell you sort of secretly, that English people are often intimidated by New Zealand homes. They always are, or mostly are, very neat and very tidy and don't look as though anybody had ever lived in them at all. This sort of worries the English, because they generally have houses that actually look very much lived in.

This is very much an obsession with Margaret. I think in quite a number of her books she feels that well-kept tidiness works counter to the imaginative sort of lateral thinking.

Margaret has this wonderful story called *Ultraviolet Catastrophe*, about an old man who's being looked after by his daughter. She really goes to great lengths to keep everything very neat and tidy. But her father feels like one of her pot plants that she waters and puts out in the sun. To keep from turning into one of her pot plants, he sings to himself or uses long words like "ultraviolet catastrophe" or "seismological singularity."

Mahy returns to the theme of the elderly in *Making Friends*, a recent picture book about two lonely old people whose dogs introduce them to one another and so they strike up a friendship.

I wish Dent would reprint one of my own favorite books of hers, *The Wind Between the Stars,* but they never have. I think it is a wonderful treatment of death. If I had to talk with a child about a bereavement, this is the book I would give them. You can read that book to quite a young child. Of course, it doesn't have to be read aloud.

I think that's a beautiful story and Brian Froud's illustrations are just lovely. I don't understand why Dent hasn't reprinted that story of death. You'll notice Margaret also talks about the neatness and tidiness and coldness of Miss Gibbs's house in this book.

Well, getting back to the old age and death theme, another book, which won the New Zealand Esther Glen Award, was *Elephant Rock* by Caroline Macdonald. That was an extraordinarily brave book to write. She deals beautifully with the story of a teenage girl whose mother is dying from cancer. The girl swims out to Elephant Rock and suddenly finds herself in a time slip where she goes back to relive her mother's youth.

She begins to understand that her mother had always known that her life would be short, but she would do all that she wanted to do within its span. The daughter will be able, through the time slip, to cope with the coming bereavement. Very sensitively done.

I remember being very impressed. I read it on the plane going down to Wellington when I was going to be one of the judges in a major award. Caroline Macdonald was put in for it and so I thought, my goodness, anyone who can write this well deserves the award and she got it.

The makers of AIM toothpaste sponsor a major award in New Zealand. Joy Cowley was the winner of it this year, for an absolutely lovely book, *Bow Down, Shadrach*. This again is about death, but this time it's the death of a cart horse.

This family on a farm has an old cart horse, an old Clydesdale horse. He's become a family pet and he's getting very old. The parents can see it would be cruel to leave him out for another winter. And they know he has to be put down.

But they don't like to tell the children he's going to be put down, so they tell the children he's going to a rest home for aged equestrian friends. But, of course, it is a small town and as soon as the children go to school the next day, they are told by all the children that the knacker's van was taking the cart horse off to be killed in Nelson.

The children are outraged. So they go off and they find this place where the horse is going to be put down and they rescue him. They have a terrible job getting him home, and he dies on the way. It's a wonderful story with a lovely twist at the end, but I won't tell you in case you buy it. I'm sure it will be taken in the States because it is such a delightful story.

The thing which was damaged was the relationship between the parents and children. The parents told their children a lie and the children were not trusting them any longer, although the lie was told with the best of intentions. Although it deals with death, it doesn't have a morbid tone, really. It's an absolutely delightful book.

I mentioned that a new or relatively newly settled country seems to go more for realism than for fantasy. The States were after all quite late in developing writers like Madeleine L'Engle and Ursula Le Guin within the history of your children's literature.

Australia has only relatively recently gotten into children's fantasy with people like Patricia Wrightson. I think she's an outstanding writer and her books, her Wirrun trilogy, have managed synthesis between the Aboriginal native material and the European, and the weaving together of the two different strands.

I don't think we've achieved that in New Zealand. The Maori remain very much the Maori in the legends and the Maori picture books and the Europeans remain the Europeans.

Recently, in the past two years, authors have come up like Gaelyn Gordon. In books like *Tales from Another Now* she is actually achieving something of a synthesis. Maybe we're gradually getting towards a state where the Maori and the European traditions are coming closer together.

If there is going to be a major theme, a distinctive thing about the New Zealand fantasy story, I would say it's going to be centered on the sea because after all our major cities are close to the sea. The sea is part of the New Zealand psyche.

Falter Tom and the Water Boy is a classic that was written in 1950 by Maurice Duggan, a well-known adult author, who has since died rather young, unfortunately.

Here again we have an old man. *Falter Tom* had been given his nickname because of a stiff leg which gave him a peculiar gait. He was an old sailor who met a water boy, who lived in the sea and invited Falter Tom to come down to live with him in the sea. Falter Tom had to get several charms in order to go down beneath the sea. At the end, he has to decide whether to go home or to stay in the sea. But finally he decides he will stay.

The sea features strongly in Joy Cowley's award winning book *The Silent One*, a wonderful story based in Polynesia. A deaf and mute young boy, who comes to land, was found in a boat and he's looked after. But when a typhoon comes and the island suffers, everybody says that he is responsible because he came in such a strange way.

It's a sort of ghostly story as he goes away to sea again and turns into a great white turtle going back to sea. Beautifully told.

The lure of the sea is central to Margaret Mahy's book, *The Man Whose Mother Was a Pirate*, which was originally published in 1960. A revised edition was published a year or two ago. The original version has quite a lot of text along with lovely pictures, but there is very good balance between text and pictures. The revised edition has a lot of pictures and not much text, which says something about the influence of television. I think the rhythm and the richness of language has lost a lot in the second edition.

I wonder what this is saying about education and children's vocabulary and everything else when a book that was so beautifully poetic and beautifully balanced was altered like that in a way that is completely unnecessary. Especially with a writer who was very established in the way that Margaret Mahy is.

One of New Zealand best contributions to children's writing is the little books that are so appropriate to learning to read by reading, which Dr. Marie Clay and Dorothy Butler have been involved in. Joy Cowley, Margaret Mahy and Ron Bacon write very much for that series. They seem to have endlessly fertile imaginations.

Until the late 1960s most New Zealand books seemed to be set in the country. The impression others have of New Zealand is that we all live on sheep farms because that was the prime residence in most New Zealand stories. When we were back in England at the end of last year, I said something to someone about living in New Zealand. And she said, "Do you ever get lonely living so far away from everybody?"

I said we do actually live in a city with a million people. In fact, only an eighth of New Zealand's population lives in the country. Now you begin to see an emergence of the cities as settings in children's literature. This has happened in the relatively last few years. I think we were all very relieved when Tessa Duder brought out modern books set in the city. Her books *Jellybean* and *Night Race to Kawau* are both set in Auckland. *Night Race to Kawau* is about a sailing ship, which is very much the Auckland scene. I was always

astonished there were not more stories about the actual
sailing.

Tessa Duder's most famous books, which are set mostly
in Auckland, are about Alex, a high achieving girl, interested
in everything: music and drama and academic work and
swimming. Alex wants to represent New Zealand at the
Olympic games, and the book recounts the trials and
problems she encounters before her goal is achieved.

One must say New Zealand seems to do well out of
proportion to its size in sports and the arts. I mean we are
only the size of one European city, three million people here.
So it's quite surprising we do get gold medals. And that we
do have Kiri Te Kanawa who's a top opera singer, Margaret
Mahy who wins all sorts of prizes, and Keri Hulme who
won the British Booker prize. I think actually it may be the
work ethic turned into the sort of drive which drives people
on, particularly in sports.

William Taylor's book *The Worst Soccer Team Ever* is a
very amusing book about sports. I think he's taking the
mystique out of this great sport image everybody likes to talk
about. Here's a boy who says they ought to just play the
game for fun and to have a team for those who aren't very
good at sports.

And, of course, the whole thing heightens when a very
feminist girl who's only 12 comes to a sports meeting at
school and insists that she be allowed to play soccer, not
netball. The book is a sort of amusing send up of school and
sports.

I think there's an anti-war theme to some of these
modern New Zealand books, which probably shows the
influence of our tremendously fluid population. New
Zealanders go overseas and quite often stop there for many,
many years. We have a son in the south of England, at the
moment. There are many people coming into New Zealand.
Perhaps many of the immigrants are keenly aware of what
was wrong with their own country, particularly war.

New Zealand, as you probably know, has a very strong
anti-nuclear stance, which has not made us very popular
with some countries, including the USA. This stance has
brought us into prominence because we have refused entry

into our ports for all ships that are nuclear powered or are carrying nuclear weapons.

A number of New Zealand books have surfaced on armed conflict. Now at the junior level, one of my favorite books is *The Duck in the Gun* by Joy Cowley. I don't know if it's published in the States.

The general and his men marched into town ready for war. When they discovered a duck had made a nest in the big gun, they decided to postpone the war until the eggs hatched. They stayed in town, and when their funds ran low, got jobs painting up the town. When the ducklings hatched and the soldiers could resume the war, they did not want to, because it would mess up all the freshly painted buildings. Besides, the general had become rather fond of the mayor's daughter. So they called off the war. A lovely comment on actual war, isn't it.

One of our very best writers is Barry Faville, a very interesting writer and I think a very fine stylist. His first book was called *The Keeper* and that was set after a nuclear holocaust. People had become very conformist, almost into tribes. The story is told by a young man who has become a scribe in order to preserve some written record of the past.

His book *The Return* tells about some people from outer space who come to a small New Zealand settlement to conduct a genetic experiment in thought transfer. Some years afterwards, a mother and son return to see how the experiment was going on.

They could detect a sudden advance in what humans were capable of achieving, but they did not know whether the new knowledge was a result of evolution or the genetic experiment. The most distressing development was the sudden appearance of a wide variety of weapons with vast destructive power. Although these new weapons were an example of technological advances, they also raised a fear about the state of mind of a race that so easily created and used them.

Sheila Jordan's book *Rocco* which won the AIM award last year, also has a background on what might happen here in nuclear war. I don't want to tell you anything more about this book, because it has such an unexpected ending that I wouldn't like to spoil it in any way.

Conservation is also a frequent element in a lot of children's books, particularly in young picture books which are not my brief tonight. We have such a significant threat to our wildlife and birds, because people are always wanting to take them away. There's a great market, I believe, for all these rather rare animals.

Several of Joan de Hamel's books have highlighted that particular problem of conservation. One of her books, *The Third Eye,* is about the threat to New Zealand native wildlife, the tuatara in this case, which is being taken away for study.

Just a word about my own books. I have already mentioned *A Sea Change: 145 Years of New Zealand Junior Fiction.* Teachers are always asking when am I going to update *A Sea Change,* which was first published in 1982. Well, I've updated a few chapters. I've also updated the chapter on children's literature in *The Oxford History of New Zealand Literature,* but that was a more academic piece.

Another of my books is *Introducing Margaret Mahy,* a biography for children. Margaret didn't want an adult biography. But she was happy to have one which she could refer children to, when they wrote to ask what people want to know about authors. That was successful in the schools here.

Before I started it, I actually did a survey of 200 New Zealand children about what they would want to know about an author. They wanted to know things like what were their favorite foods and their favorite authors, what did they do when they were children, what influenced their writing and so on.

I'll let you in on a bit of a secret. We've found it quite difficult to get through to teachers. They don't read reviews and they don't always go to book shops. The best way to get to teachers actually is by publishing a book for children. So I wrote *Twenty-One New Zealand Children's Writers.*

I took the format I used in the Margaret Mahy book and put the questions in a box with a picture of the author. Then I've done an essay about the author that really says the sort of things I've said tonight. At the end of the chapter each author has a complete bibliography.

Ostensibly I wrote it for children, because I wanted it to get into the schools so that children would see it. Having written for a wide-readership newspaper for many years, I knew I had to keep a fairly accessible approach. That means the book is very readable to children by the age nine onwards. So you see one doesn't have to make much difference in vocabulary to reach both audiences.

When I finished that book at the end of last year, I went to talk at a famous girls' public school in York, England. I thought I'd go into one of the book shops beforehand to see if they had any books by New Zealand authors. When I went into the Puffin Book shop, I was astonished to find books on the shelves by 15 of the 21 authors I'd profiled. But I don't think many people realized they were actually New Zealand authors. I just wonder how many of those authors are also in the U.S. book shops.

I had fun compiling *Under the Rainbow*, which is a treasury of New Zealand children's stories. Because last year was our 150th anniversary, I decided to arrange the anthology so that it also is the story of New Zealand.

It began with a story by Margaret Mahy called *Thunderstorms and Rainbows,* which is about New Zealand's stormy weather. Next, we had a retelling of a Maori legend and then something about Captain Cook, who discovered New Zealand, and a story about the whalers. It finished up with contemporary New Zealand stories, like *Night Race to Kawau* by Tessa Duder.

I think if we have a weakness in New Zealand it's in illustration and that's partly due to the predominance of abstract expressionism, which has meant that less time is devoted to drawing in art schools. My husband could talk about this. He lectures in fine arts.

Gavin Bishop is an exception. He's developed a style of his own and he does know what he's after, as does Robin Belton, who has a lovely style. But I do think New Zealand illustration and book production sometimes does a disservice to the author.

I frankly think some of Dorothy Butler's books have been done a considerable disservice by the illustrations she has been given. Did you see the picture book about the baby? I thought the text was lovely, but I thought the

illustrations did not do it justice. And I would say that
happens more often than not.

I think Margaret Mahy's books have always been so
beautifully produced with very fine British or U.S.
illustrators. I don't think any of her books have been
published first in New Zealand. She has always published
first in England and in the States. Then they're actually
brought to New Zealand. In fact, at one time they sold out
and we didn't get them here.

Something similar happened very much in the 1930s.
Some of the classics by top New Zealand writers like Esther
Glen were always published overseas in Britain. Very often
their books didn't get here. So New Zealanders didn't know
New Zealand classics, actually. Interesting.

My husband and I did a joint picture book which will
come out in November. I don't like the title at all, but the
English publisher insisted on our changing it from *The
Bigger Digger* to *The Little Yellow Digger* ; and because we
in New Zealand are so dependent on overseas publishers
taking our books, we have to comply with their wishes.

Well, I think I'm coming to a conclusion.

I have been in this field since 1972 and I can truthfully
say when I started, the best books were coming from
overseas. But in the past 10 years or so, I believe the books
we have from Australia and New Zealand are as good, if not
better, than many of the books we get from overseas, and I
say that very dispassionately. I think we are getting our own
identity. Our own literature is very much together.

The great problem, which has hit New Zealand authors,
is trying to get overseas publishers to accept their books. A
book is not often going to get a print run of many more than
2,000 copies here. Well, this doesn't make many royalties.
So if they want to make money on their book, they really
need to get it taken by publishing firms in the United States
and Britain.

Our authors are having awful problems with some
publishers, particularly US publishers who say, "Well, you
can't have this, because our children wouldn't understand
this word." Now New Zealand children grew up with the
knowledge that we call a sidewalk a *pavement*, but

Americans call it a *sidewalk*, and they understand the two terms.

I can remember reading *Anne of Green Gables* and wondering what clam chowder was. I didn't really know what clam chowder was until I went to Canada last year. But I knew it was something Canadians ate, and I thought it was rather interesting. I didn't have to actually know or understand every word to appreciate a book from another country.

Our children read the American Laura Ingalls Wilder and English historical novels, but we would not be able to get *our* books about New Zealand history taken by overseas publishers. So this is really creating a fiscal dilemma for the New Zealand writer. If you have to write everything international, as it were, then, to some extent, you're losing your New Zealand identity. You see the problem and it's a very real one.

DOROTHY BUTLER

Dorothy Butler is a teacher, critic, and former book shop owner, as well as an author. Her first book, *Cushla and Her Books,* was her graduate thesis, which was based on the strong, positive influence of books on her granddaughter, who has severe, multiple handicaps. She knows books intimately and is a passionate advocate for parents reading to young children. Recently, she has ventured into writing picture books. We traveled through an awesomely beautiful temperate rain forest to Dorothy Butler's home. The bus wound upward on a curving road, which has only been paved for a few years, and finally down a cliff-like road to the coast.

My daughter is here today, which means I'm not likely to exaggerate too wildly. She may even interrupt me. One group of people you can't deceive are your children.

So many people have asked about Karekare and Winchelsea House, which is this house that you're in, that I think perhaps I should start by telling you about it. This land with the two houses was, for some time before we bought it, a guest house complex. It was built more than 100 years ago in old, original kauri wood. The paneling is a lovely, buttery color.

This was the first house out on this particular piece of the Tasman coast. It was built by a very famous man called Charles Primrose Murdoch, who built a railway between Karekare and Whatipu, some miles around the rocky coast, to take out the kauri logs. This was an extraordinary thing for him to do and an outstanding engineering feat.

When Charles Murdoch lived here with his wife and 10 children, the house was at least twice as big as it is now. The rest of it was pulled down before our time, and the house next door was built.

We had to restore this house because it was registered as being of historic significance. We do let it out sometimes. We work on the principle that if we can make enough each year to pay the rates and a little bit for upkeep, that's about all we can hope for. You'll be interested to hear that we've had plenty of lovely Americans and Japanese and all sorts of people here, over the years.

The house next door is where Cushla was brought up. Most of you will know the story of Cushla, through the book which was written about her, which was really my graduate thesis.

Cushla is now 20 years of age. She was a child with multiple handicaps. The book was written about her very early development through books, which was, and continues to be, phenomenal.

She is a person of both physical and intellectual handicaps, and the fact that she can speak, read and write as she does is quite out of proportion to what was thought to be possible. Now that she's grown up, she's associating with handicapped people. Many people her own age, who are not actually as handicapped as Cushla, don't have her capacities.

I always feel that Cushla's story strikes a real blow for books. In fact, the greater her handicaps can be proven to be (and they are considerable), the more I feel we can believe in the power of books and of reading to children. She's not there at the moment, but will be tonight. I'm afraid you have just missed her.

Anyway, we bought this place about 20 years ago when Cushla was a baby. All three houses belonged to us, and her young parents planned to live in one of them with this badly handicapped baby. Later, they bought their home from us.

Now, as usual, I'm not quite sure what you want me to talk about. I could talk forever about my own books and writing and the way I came to be an author. I would say I became an author accidentally. I didn't have a book published until I was—let's see, I was born in 1925 and my first book was published in 1979, so you can see I was well into my 50s.

That doesn't mean that I didn't write. I wrote all the time, from the time I was about so big. I grew up in the depression in New Zealand, in a working class family. I was blessed, I now see, with a mother who, although not well educated herself, was an intelligent person. My mother realized, that from an early age, what Dorothy wanted more than anything on earth was plenty of paper. And she literally used to buy paper for me, when it was hard to find money for food and clothes.

There was not a lot of paper in those days and certainly not in working class families. Now, everywhere you look there's paper, and it is hard to believe that it was hard to come by, but it was. If someone wanted to write something in an ordinary household, finding a writing pad would be quite difficult. That would have been true for many people.

Whereas, I always had paper. I always wrote books. My father was a butcher and he used to bring home for me the ends of the rolls of brown paper that they wrapped meat in. I used to cut them out and make tiny little books which I stitched together. Nobody had invented cello-tape. I stitched these little books by hand, and then wrote stories in them.

I became addicted to books as a child—to the sight and feel and smell of them. In my family, although books were not in abundant supply, they were read. We had that shelf of classics, common in many homes at that time. I read these from a very early age, only half understanding; but something of the strength and structure of well-fashioned prose must have seeped into my bones and remained, because I still love those old books.

When I was at school I learned very quickly, simply because I could always read. My mother said I was born knowing how to read, which I think is an exaggeration. Nonetheless, I always did well in that particular sphere at school.

I turned my back on everything else and didn't want to do the other things in school, but I always loved anything that involved reading and writing. I was also a very vigorous outdoor sort of child. The two together seemed to give me a pretty good life.

By the skin of my teeth, I got to university in a part-time capacity. There was no chance in those days for someone from a family such as mine to be a full-time student in university. But I managed to get a degree and get myself trained as a teacher.

I was married about the time I finished university. At the end of my first year of teaching, I had our first child. Of course, in those days, it wasn't really respectable to teach when one was obviously pregnant. But also in those days in

secondary schools in New Zealand, we had to wear
academic gowns. And academic gowns were marvelous for
covering up.

We then proceeded, rather recklessly, to have a very
large family of children, six daughters and two sons. I was
always more interested in their books, from the time they
were born, than virtually any other aspect of their lives.

I'm addicted to babies and small children, anyway. I
can't resist them. This has continued, and fortunately, my
children have obliged by providing me with very large
numbers of delectable and toothsome grandchildren.

From the time that Catherine, our first child, was born, I
was collecting books. In those days, of course, in New
Zealand, we would have had Beatrix Potter, *The Wind in the
Willows, Winnie the Pooh* and *Peter Pan* but not much
more.

But change was on the way. A marvelous woman called
Dorothy Neal White went to the Carnegie Institute in
Pittsburgh to study library science and came back to New
Zealand and wrote a book called *About Books for Children.*

I can remember this appearing when I was training as a
teacher; and it was a miraculous thing, that book, because no
books had been published in New Zealand for the whole of
the war. It must have been one of the first books (1946, I
think it was) after the war.

It was a book that actually became famous in America,
too. In fact, I'm sure American libraries would still have old
copies. Then, bless her heart, Dorothy Neal White, wrote a
book called *Books Before Five,* just in time for me. That
became one of the books I loved, and read and read, until I
literally knew parts of it by heart.

In fact, I've had great trouble over the years when I'm
talking to people. Sometimes I will say something, and then
think to myself, "I think that was plagiarism. That wasn't
me. That was Dorothy Neal White."

This was a great, good fortune. Because of this book,
New Zealand booksellers and libraries started bringing in
American books. My children grew up with *Madeline.* In
fact, I have a lovely little granddaughter called Madeline.
Mike Mulligan was another favorite. (And I have a grandson
called Michael!) We had rows and rows of books.

My daughter is looking in from the kitchen. I'm sure she could give you quite a list. They were all American books, you see, in American editions. This doesn't happen now. We don't have American books here very often, unless a particular bookseller goes to enormous trouble to bring them in individually. They don't come as a group, as they did in those days.

As soon as they could, our children joined the library. To begin with, they and their father used to trek from the North Shore right over to the Auckland Public Library most Friday nights. This involved a bus trip and a ferry trip and quite a long walk in order to get those marvelous books.

And then the Birkenhead Library opened in our suburb on the North Shore. I think they opened the door and the Butler family fell in! We were original subscribers to that library, and our children always loved to make trips there.

I've always been a person who wrote things down, details of what I'd been reading and so forth. I still do. I started keeping catalogs of the books we were reading, noting details about those which came our way from libraries, schools, and other sources. Years later, these catalogs proved invaluable.

When my two youngest children and I joined the Playcentre movement, I decided to train as a supervisor. Playcentre is a parent co-operative movement, which is very strong in New Zealand. I would say it has been one of our leading educational feats. It dates back to the 1940s, when it started training parents to run their own early childhood centers.

Playcentre trains parents, not only in a practical way, but in a truly academic way. This academic training is available to young parents, who may have virtually no book-learning themselves to begin with, or may have academic qualifications. Through my work with such parents, I discovered that adults who are ignorant of the intricacies of literary criticism can easily learn the features of a successful story if they read it with a group of young children. The best books can be invigorating, ultimately producing readers who respond to the world with readiness to wonder, to love, and to laugh, and parents soon realize this.

If there's one thing in this world I've seen really work, it's the Playcentre movement of New Zealand. And, of course, people have come from all parts of the world, including America, to study it.

It became quite quickly known that I was something of an authority on young children's books. This was a very easy thing to be. It was like being a very big fish in a very little bowl, you know. There were not too many people who were knowledgeable in the field.

From this point onwards, I was asked to teach or give lectures on the subject by the university's Continuing Education Department. I also did some consulting work for teachers colleges and, almost accidentally, I fell into having a book shop.

Now this is what I mean about accidental. During my years in Playcentre, I developed a system whereby I used to sell books on behalf of any book shop in town, who was willing to let me have them. The adults at the Playcentre became interested in buying books of their own after watching the happy interaction of young children, parents, and good books.

I met this demand as well as I could, picking up books from Auckland booksellers, who would give me a 10 percent discount. Then I'd spend this 10 percent on buying books for the Playcentre. That meant our center eventually had the best library in Auckland, if not in the whole of New Zealand.

As a result, I got to know a lot of publishers. They would send me books and ask if I would include them on the Playcentre lists.

One of them once said to me—it was a dear man called David Mackie—"Why don't you take books straight from us, Dorothy? We'd sell them to you wholesale and that would be much cheaper than getting them from the book shops." And I said, "But do you mean I'd be *selling* them to the parents?" And he said, "Yes." Then I said, "But I'd be making a profit"—almost as if there was something dirty about that.

At this point, I thought I was going back to teaching. I was already doing evening teaching at the secondary level—

you call it high school—several nights a week and teaching at the technical institute in Auckland.

We had eight children, all growing up and needing support of one sort or another, not the least financial. I did need to make a bit of extra money. Then I started to realize how involved I became with my evening school students. I thought to myself, "Goodness, full-time teaching when we have all these children of our own. I'll become so involved, it will be impossible. Perhaps a little book venture would be a good idea."

I can remember my husband, Roy, saying to me when I mentioned it to him, "Well, as long as it doesn't actually cost us money." Of course, for awhile it did. We put a little bit of money into it, and we counted on paying for the books with the money that came in. We were running up the down escalator for awhile! But the business flourished.

I then became very interested in learning more about the acquisition of reading skills. In fact, I've always been obsessed with this subject. I still am. I read everything that comes out. I keep hoping somebody will make a real breakthrough. Of course, they do make little breakthroughs all the time into the acquisition of reading and the reason some children, even children from very bookish backgrounds, still have difficulties.

I decided I'd go back to a university and do some more subjects. I had originally done English literature and that sort of thing. So I started doing a postgraduate degree called a Diploma in Education. As part of this, I had to do what they called an "original investigation," which is actually a small thesis. You had three years to do this, and you had to enroll each year.

I don't mean that it had to take three years, but you had to produce it within three years. I did my "original investigation" about Cushla in the last six months of the third year!

I didn't really need another paper qualification, but I'd collected all this material about the influence of reading on Cushla's development. Rather, my daughter, Patricia, had. She had a great box of all of Cushla's records and I had my own collection.

I thought I would use all this material, although I thought they might not even accept it as a thesis. But still it would get me down to organizing it, and that was what I wanted to do.

Some of the material is encrusted from jellied fingers. You know, marmite, honey, and whatever. Patricia would be at the breakfast table frantically scribbling down what Cushla said.

Cushla's tests had been done at Auckland University and her physical tests had been done at Auckland Hospital, which is a teaching hospital. So all this material chronicling Cushla's development during her first five years was absolutely authentic. Marie Clay—most of you will know her as a famous educator—had always taken an interest in Cushla.

The records describe the strong impact of books and stories on her personal development and her acquisition of literacy. (Several of my librarian friends have said that I must deliver the box of records some day, so it will go into some sort of archive.)

Well, of course, choosing that topic for my independent investigation was another accident. Once it was done, three bound copies with photos and charts and graphs, and heaven only knows what, were delivered to the University of Auckland that summer. I thought, "Well, that's done." And I put it out of my mind.

From that point, several publishers heard about it, because, of course, it was in the postgraduate library and teachers kept taking it out. One of them called Helen Dupree, who incidentally has done quite a lot of teaching recently in America, was married to a publisher called Alan Dupree. She thrust it upon him and insisted it should be published. Of course, I knew nothing about this at all.

I already knew Alan, however, and he rang me and asked if I'd mind if he submitted it for publication. I was doubtful. Then various others called. And I turned down several offers which came from England. I imagined the whole thing being given a sort of *Reader's Digest* treatment, you know. And I couldn't abide the idea of that.

Some of my articles had already been published in England. The publishers of *Signal Magazine* asked me if they might publish the book list part of the thesis, and I saw no reason whatsoever why they shouldn't do that. That started the train. I had already agreed to Alan Dupree's offer to send it to Hodder and Stoughton in England, with the proviso that it must not be altered. Ultimately, *Cushla* went into an American edition and was translated into Japanese.

At that point, The Bodley Head in London asked me if I'd write *Babies Need Books*. When they asked me this, I, in my ignorance, didn't even think that this was a surprising thing for them to do. Because, of course, they could have asked anybody at all in England.

It was meant to be an English book. And it was made clear to me it was to be an English book, describing English children's books. It was to be a book coming out of London, not coming out of Auckland. Therefore, a New Zealand book would go into it only as it could hold its head up on the world market.

Of course, at that time as I say, I didn't realize it was remarkable and I said, "Yes, I would do this." And I did do it. And, of course, from that point, we were away. Marie Clay and I did together *Reading Begins at Home*, which is a New Zealand book. There is an American edition, which has sold very well, too. It's been revised twice. I've done the revisions. The latest edition has had an American do the book lists at the back.

Then I did *Five Through Eight* which I think is my favorite book, although it never went into an American edition. I've had more letters from people who have found this book useful, I think, even than *Babies Need Books*.

In an odd sort of way, it's the one I enjoy most when I reread it. Those of you who have written something will know exactly what I mean. You get to the stage where you pick up an article you wrote 20 years ago and it's as if you're reading something somebody else wrote. And you are absolutely objectively able to either shiver slightly and think, "Good lord, did I do that?" or "That was a bit over the top." or "Wasn't that good?"

Meanwhile, they had asked me in England to do a collection of New Zealand stories, and I can remember saying I wouldn't sign a contract for this. I wasn't sure that I could, because I wanted it to be almost definitive, if you know what I mean. I wasn't going to do it unless it could include all of the very best people. Ultimately, it did. It's called *The Magpies Said.*

When you run your eye down the list of authors included in the collection, you will see all the famous New Zealand children's writers. It has, for example, the very first published piece of work by Tessa Duder. I worked with Tessa on that story, so there's quite a lot of me in it, too. Tessa had this wonderful tendency to go racing off on a tangent. She could always write, but she had to learn to prune her work severely. She and I have often talked about this. Now, of course, she is one of our most successful authors. I'm very proud of her.

Magpies has a Margaret Mahy, which would have been an early one. It also has Sam Hunt, who is almost our national poet, and, of course, Katherine Mansfield and Elsie Locke and Joy Cowley. Everybody in America knows Joy Cowley, surely, Eve Sutton, Dennis Glover, Morris Duggan, Barry Faville. I managed to get a story out of all of those people.

It took me about three years literally extorting something from them. I feel that it is a real gem. I didn't write a word of it, so I can say this without being thought immodest. It was done in a beautiful hardback, but, unfortunately, that went out of print. It was in print in paperback for some years. But that has now gone out of print, too, and there's nothing I can do about it.

They assure me at Penguin that they will bring it back some day. I think they're waiting to bring it back as a sort of period piece. I can tell when it was written, because it has a list of grandchildren in it. And it has on the bottom—"And other grandchildren to come." There are 10 listed and there are now 20.

The eldest one, who is called Nicola, told me she was coming home from school one day just after this book was published and she saw a little display of it in a Brown's Bay book shop window. She said to the friend she was with— she was about 11, she's now 24,—"I'm in that book. That book's dedicated to me and all my cousins. And my grandmother wrote it." Her friend scoffed, "Aw, go on."

So, with great alacrity, they went in and looked at it. Nicola was able to open it up at the front and show her friend her name at the top of the list. I do love that one.

Now I've got to the stage where I do some reviewing and a bit of visiting lecturing and teaching, and I visit local schools. In fact, every day of the week I could be going to schools and reading to children. But I'd never really get anything else done if I did that.

I run a library for the children who go to the little local school using my own books, in my home. This little school has 15 children at the moment and four of them are my grandchildren.

I'm having a lovely time writing children's picture book texts, and I regard that as total self-indulgence. In fact, I have so many that haven't even been published yet, that I think I should stop writing. But then I think "Why stop?" because I actually write them for fun. I truly do think I've got to the stage of life where I may as well do the things I enjoy most. So that is what I'm doing.

Recently I was asked to write a few little school readers. I'm not very good at writing passionless texts. And I can't do what Joy Cowley can. She can somehow get great spirit and punch into just the fewest words you can imagine.

That obviously isn't my thing. I am inclined to be wordy. That's partly because that's how I like children's lives to be, filled with a sort of wordiness. I feel as if it's so good for small children to be exposed to a lot of words, and not just the simple, obvious ones.

I'm told there was an early edition of "Peter Rabbit" in America in which they changed "the little birds implored Peter to exert himself" to "they told him to try harder" or something like that. Well, "imploring someone to exert themselves" seems to me the way it ought to be!

Several people here have shown interest in the sequel to my book *A Happy Tale,* which was bought by an American publisher. However, they did not take the sequel, *Another Happy Tale.* Apparently, they did not like the way I let the baby get muddled up with the pigs. A rather over-earnest response, I thought!

It's the story of Mabel and Ned who lived with their new baby on a tiny farm in the middle of a large island. If you read the first book, you'll discover that Mabel has actually joined Ned because she fell out of an airplane—quite ridiculous and the whole thing is meant to be farcical. If we can't have a bit of nonsense in life...

Mabel was not very good at looking after babies. Ned was very good at looking after animals, so he offered to look after the baby, too. I think that was supposed to be a little bit unprincipled.

He seemed to think that babies could actually look after themselves as baby animals did. The baby begins to spend most of its time with the pigs and is accidentally sent off to market with them. Of course, all is well in the end.

I also am continuing the series of books based on my mother's life growing up at the turn of the century in the old gold-mining town of Thames. The first is called *By Jingo.* I began to write the second book for the six through nine age group, but now that I've written one chapter and a bit of the next, I can see it's really for nine to 12 year-olds.

Once again, I'm doing this just because I enjoy doing it. I'd like to see it published, if I ever get it finished. There's no guarantee, of course, but the person who has published the earlier books has already rung me up and urged me on. So that's where I am at the moment—with a contract from Penguin Books in London for a third revised edition of *Babies Need Books,* as well. With my large family, garden and involvement with books, my life is very full and happy.

TESSA DUDER

Tessa Duder is an author of children's and young adult's novels, whose best-known novels, about Alex, reflect the author's love of swimming. *Alex*, the first book in the series, is Penguin New Zealand's all-time biggest seller and has been made into a movie. Houghton Mifflin has published some of the *Alex* books in the United States as sports fiction under the title *In Lane Three, Alex Archer.* Story tour travelers felt this was too narrow a definition for these books that are used as texts in many New Zealand schools. Readers sometimes assume the *Alex* books, with their three-dimensional, multi-talented heroine, are autobiographical. Mrs. Duder told us why they are not, when we visited her at the Jabberwocky Book Shop in Auckland.

I'm highly delighted you're here in New Zealand and particularly in Auckland in my favorite shop, the Jabberwocky Book Shop. Jo Noble, the owner, is known throughout New Zealand as an authority on children's books.

We in Auckland are extremely well served to have two children's book shops which are run by highly authoritative people. Dorothy Butler started the other shop which goes back probably 20 years now. This shop has been running for 12 years.

Of course, you all met Dorothy this morning. You must have dragged yourselves away with some difficulty, because she is such an enormously interesting person and knowledgeable about children's books. I have a particular debt to Dorothy for her help when I was just starting.

In 1978 my youngest daughter had just started going to school. So here I was with a small period of time each day after 11 years of nappies and caring for four very young daughters. Although a long, long time ago I had been a journalist both in Auckland and in London, I wasn't really thinking about writing.

Children often ask me when or how I became a writer. The question is actually wrong. I didn't decide to become a

33

writer. My first story chose me. For some reason that I have no knowledge of, it came to me in the middle of the night.

I began to wonder what happens when a family goes sailing and the father knocks himself out with the spinnaker boom. The children and the mother have to continue on through the night with the rising wind. They don't believe they are particularly competent sailors. In the past, they left all the main decisions to their father. Now he is lying unconscious on the deck. So what happens to the yacht and the family? The only way for me to find out was to sit down and write the book. So I did.

About halfway through—no, that's not strictly true—after six months, I had a crisis of confidence. At that point I joined the Children's Literature Association. The association is a wonderful body of collaboration among teachers, librarians, some writers, some illustrators, some booksellers and parents. All members are professionally, or as parents, interested in good books for children. It was started about 25 years ago in Auckland and since has spread to other centers.

The best thing I did in 1978 was to join that organization. Through that, I summoned up courage to approach Dorothy Butler and ask her to read the manuscript I'd been working on. She often read manuscripts for aspiring writers and also did a lot of reading for publishers. She agreed to do it as a professional commission for a fee.

It was the best $50 I ever spent, because her assessment was very wise. She did say, very realistically, "This is not publishable standard, but you do have some talent." She told me to throw away the 60,000 words I'd already written. Then she said the very fact that I had written 30,000 words, and not even come to the main point of the story, indicated I had some talent in holding a reader, which was quite a nice way of putting it.

So I have a particular reverence for and a particular relationship with Dorothy because she was the first person who ever saw any of my fiction.

I never had done any creative writing other than two or three attempts in school a long time ago. When I went through school, there was very little done in fiction. We wrote very boring essays on given topics and had very little freedom or encouragement to write our own stories in New Zealand in the 1950s. Things have changed considerably.

So Dorothy looked at this manuscript for a novel and three or four short stories I'd written. As luck would have it, she liked one of the short stories, called *The Violin*, enough to include it in her anthology *The Magpies Said* (Viking Kestrel, 1981).

As far as the novel goes, she told me I should stop preaching to the children. To quit telling them about not littering and leaving rubbish around and to stop carrying on about the role of women in a very didactic sort of way. She told me to throw all that away and start again.

So I did. After two-and-a-half years I had a manuscript and I knew what happened to my fictional family. The book, *Night Race to Kawau*, was published in 1982 by the New Zealand branch of Oxford University Press, which is associated with, but not really accountable to, the Oxford University Press in England.

I've been an Oxford author ever since I started. Through them I've published six novels and a nonfiction children's book, *The Story of Auckland.* Oxford is one of the smaller multinational publishers here, but it is a strong one with a regular children's list. It is not as big as it used to be, but it now has three or four children's novels in print. Unfortunately, they don't do picture books any longer. That went by the way a few years ago.

Night Race to Kawau didn't make a great impact when it came out, although it was shortlisted for the Children's Book of the Year award and was picked up by Penguin Books and brought out internationally in a Puffin edition.

There is, in fact, a night race to Kawau every year. So the book is centered on a genuine event. Kawau is a Maori word for a shag, a fishing-type sea bird. It is also the name of a small island about 30 miles north of Auckland.

Auckland is quite a center for yachting, actually. It's from here that we made our third, and I must say unsuccessful, attempt at the America's Cup earlier this year. Auckland has a very strong tradition for yachting, despite the fact that Auckland's only been operating as a city since 1840. So our history is not long, but it's pretty rich, considering that short period of time.

By the time *Night Race to Kawau* came out at the end of 1982, I'd decided I wanted to be a professional writer. I was well into my next book called *Jellybean*, which was published in 1985. Viking Kestrel published it in America.

Jellybean was included on the American Library Association list of notable books for children in 1986. Obviously, I was highly pleased about that. There are only 50 books on that list and with the vast numbers of books (somebody told me 4,000 novels come out in America every year) I felt it was a great honor to be picked.

I should also say it was one of 10 books shortlisted for a major award here. I think *Jellybean* is the only children's novel, so far, which has been shortlisted for the Goodman Fielder Wattie Book Award.

Jellybean astonishes me. It was my second book and quite a lot of people find *Jellybean* is the one they like best. It is quite a strange little book about a girl whose mother is a professional musician. At the beginning of the book, she is really very uncertain as to where she stands in her mother's life. Her mother is a cellist in an orchestra. Obviously that means she has to work a lot at night and Jellybean is left with a baby-sitter. Jellybean thinks she comes in second best to her mother's cello.

In the course of the story, she finds out quite a number of things, including the fact that she is not second best. She also sets some priorities for what she wants to do with her life.

Jellybean was a very instinctive book. I just wrote it without a lot of planning. Now that I've done the Alex books, I'm much more calculating about what I'm doing. Now I plan. I draw up charts. I do a lot of what filmmakers call back story. Terrible word, isn't it? Back story covers all the things that happen before the film starts. And back story helps you, as a writer, to know more about your characters, from the clothes they wear, to who their family was, to where they were raised, to all the things that make them an individual. I do a great deal of that now. In fact, I go overboard, because I like to know.

As a writer, I'm only doing half the work in creating characters and settings. Children always are astonished when I emphasize that they are required to do half the work of making a story live for them. They bring their own experience, their own knowledge of language, and their own particular background to whatever they read. This is the great satisfaction in reading as opposed to television or film.

Jellybean required very little editing. I learned huge amounts during that time of editing *Night Race to Kawau*. I edited it together with a very good editor, who showed me how to cut 30,000 words from an over-written manuscript. I must say that halfway through the book I was getting quite good, and by the last half, I probably edited most of it myself.

Unfortunately, quite a few authors are left out of the editing process. I think it must be quite devastating to a first-time author to hand in a book which is accepted and next thing you know it comes back to you covered with blue pencil.

The book I'm best known for is called *Alex* here. It is published in America by Houghton Mifflin under the title *In Lane Three, Alex Archer*. They wanted the title to indicate that this book came under the general category of sports fiction. So they wrote and asked me if I would mind the title change and I said no. I'm not really enthusiastic about it. But I'm pragmatic. They know the market better than I do.

Alex is actually a combination of three or four different people. I'd say that two of them are my daughters. She's also based physically on a girl I remember from my teen years.

Generally, when authors create a character, they roll up a number of people, combine them all, stir them up, put them in a hopper and come up with a new character. I think that's probably true of all my characters.

Because I was a swimmer and because I'm one of these people who likes to have fingers in quite a lot of pies, I do get accused frequently that Alex is autobiographical. I deny it absolutely. For one thing, I'm not 5 foot 10. Alex is much more assertive than I am. She's much more capable of being quite stroppy. I'm really quite a wimp. Perhaps I've written the sort of person I'd really like to be. Even though I'm not.

When I was in my mid-teens, I did represent New Zealand as a swimmer—not at the Olympic games, I have to say. But at what we used to call the Empire Games. Now we call them the Commonwealth Games. The most recent one was held in Auckland in 1990.

So in 1958 I went to London, then on to Cardiff, Wales, where the Empire Games were held. What I've obviously done is taken some of the experiences and the details of what it's like to compete in an international arena, and transferred them to the Olympic Games in Rome in 1960.

Since I didn't have direct experience in Rome, I went there when I was researching the book. I spent 10 days there just wandering around. Rome actually looks very similar now to what it was in 1960. The reason I know that is because I was given four hours of film of Rome in the 1960s, the official film of the 1960 Olympics. I was sitting there in Rome looking at that film when I thought, "This is ridiculous. This is on video. Perhaps I can get a copy of it to take back to New Zealand."

When I asked about getting a copy of the video, the man took it out of the machine and gave it to me. So I came back from my visit to Rome with four hours of absolutely priceless research material, which has all been fitted into *Alex in Rome,* also published in the USA by Houghton Mifflin.

Although it's quite a slim book, there's a huge amount of detail. I believe all the details in that book are correct, right down to what color the postage stamps were. I'm a pedantic person and I like to know that all those details are correct. Then I feel I have got a firm base on which I can build the characters.

None of the events upon which these books are built happened to me. I did not break my leg as an aspiring swimmer. I did not have fights with officials in the same way as I described. But Dawn Fraser, the great Australian swimmer of this period, had lots of fights with officials. I read her autobiography when I was researching the book. I found it very, very useful material.

I didn't have a rival in the way that I've described Maggie Benton. I certainly did know a pushy mother who was very much the model for Mrs. Benton, and I will go to my grave without saying who it is.

The pushy mother—the highly ambitious mother—we have a lot of examples. Mrs. Benton was a stereotype in a sense, but I also tried to make her a woman with some humanity. In fact, in *Alex in Winter* you do find out quite a lot about Mrs. Benton and what makes her the apparently ruthless person she is. It's a sad story—a typical story of a woman of that period. She's a woman who was never allowed to develop her own particular talents, so she pours all her ambitions back into her daughter.

One of the main bits of feedback I've had from the first Alex book continues to astonish me. Time and time again people tell me that when they get to the part of the book where Alex's boyfriend, Andy, dies, they burst into tears.

It took me about three weeks to decide that I had to kill Andy off. Suddenly, I had the power to do it. When I described Andy's death, I drew on how I felt when I was 26 years old and heard that my 16-year-old cousin had been killed in a car accident in Britain. I was living in Pakistan at the time. So it was a long way removed. Although it was not a direct experience, I think if I've drawn on anything, I've drawn on that.

The reason the story of Alex became a quartet was this voice that started in the back of my head saying "What happened? I won that race. I have a chance to go to Rome. Did I go? If I did, how did I get on?"

I resisted this voice for about three weeks. That was all. I knew I eventually had to write another book. The second book, *Alex in Winter,* takes her through both an emotional winter and a physical winter while she prepares for the 1960 Olympics.

When the summer Olympic games are held, it's winter in New Zealand. So young athletes, all athletes, had to do most of their training in the off season. These days our athletes train for the summer games overseas, in America and all over the place. But in the 1950s and 1960s, that was not an option.

When I started that second book, I knew straight off that there had to be a third. Even so, I had a real problem knowing where to stop with *Alex in Winter.* Finally, I decided to stop when she arrives in Rome, but before she takes part in the Olympics. This was a difficult decision. It meant *Alex in Winter* was going to be seen as an incomplete book. I would run the risk of losing sympathy for her as a character. I knew that. This was the main objection of the American publishers, who decided not to publish it. Possibly they thought I had run that risk and it had not come off.

The third book is called (in New Zealand) *Alessandra: Alex in Rome*. I felt if I simply had her going through the Rome games, with all the information and research I had done, the third book could become a rather boring travelogue. So I had to invent another character. In essence, a male version of Alex. A strong, assertive and very talented young man.

I invented Tom, because I wanted her experience in the Rome Olympics in 1960 to be colored by somebody who wasn't a swimmer, somebody who came from a different set of priorities and talents. Tom is a New Zealander, who is in Italy to study opera. This meant I had to get into the whole business of opera and singers.

The third book finishes with her flying away from Italy. But it wasn't originally intended to happen that way at all. It just happened. I wrote this manuscript last year when I was the first writer-in-residence at the university in Hamilton, a small inland river-bank city about 80 miles south of Auckland. I was sitting there in my office in the English Department writing this book and it got bigger and bigger. It must have had something to do with the environment.

Last May I went to Oxford with this enormous manuscript with 132,000 words. I hoped they would bring it out in one book. But for commercial reasons, I knew that they probably couldn't. I really did know in my heart of hearts.

Eventually, it came out as two books. The third book was published last October and the fourth in March. Both of them have been on the national best seller list against all the adult books since then. I'm pleased to say there is a huge readership for the Alex books.

Houghton Mifflin is publishing the third book, *Alessandra: Alex in Rome*, in America in the fall. Rather surprisingly, they're waiting to decide whether to publish the fourth book, *Songs for Alex*, until they see how the third one goes. I was rather dismayed and also rather flattered, because that means the third book actually does stand on its own as a satisfying book.

Of course, as a writer that's a problem you always have writing what is basically going to become a quartet. The conventions say each of these four books has to be readable by itself. You should be able to read the third book without reading the first one. But, obviously, the third book will be a lot richer if you've read the first two.

I'm surprised by their decision, because the third book finishes with Alex flying back to New Zealand after the games in Rome. Her relationship with Tom is by no means resolved, and it doesn't get resolved until the very last pages of the fourth book.

The last book, which by the way is not very easy to read, is called *Songs for Alex*. Alex has the sort of withdrawal young athletes go through after a major event. I always knew where this one was going to finish. It follows her for six months as she copes with being a celebrity and tries to get back to normal life.

In a sense, the fourth book is like the first book. Both are about a young person making choices and deciding what paths she ought to take. Alex makes all sorts of crucial decisions about whether she's going to continue with this sport which has meant so much to her for the last six years or whether she wants to go back to school for her final year or whether she wants to go straight on for university.

She has to decide whether to accept a four-year swimming scholarship at a prestigious American university, possibly one in California. Of course, that would mean she has to make a four-year commitment. So she won't do that.

Alex actually gets a chance to play St. Joan in George Bernard Shaw's play. It's a part that takes great courage and would be a dream part for any young woman, particularly one of Alex's stroppy nature. This book includes a great deal about Joan of Arc and those three years in which she rose out of obscurity to become a legend.

It seemed to me there were some parallels with Alex's life and with the sort of person she was and what she could bring to that part when she played it. I did a lot of reading— in fact a lot of what I read went into that. Because I didn't feel terribly comfortable writing about a theatrical experience without any sort of help, I spoke to two actresses who had played St. Joan. They read my book quite early to make sure I wasn't making any drastic amateurish errors.

The extraordinary thing about this is that I thought I'd never get up on a stage again when I wrote this book. It had been 30 years since I'd had any theatrical experience at all. About three months after I finished this book, I had a chance to be in a performance of *Twelfth Night*. That was really rather an extraordinary experience because quite a lot of things that happened in the book happened six months later. Odd, very odd indeed.

Alex has been published in three other international editions. The Catalan edition, *La cursa final,* which means *The Final Race,* came out about two years ago. This book was set in 1959 and the cover shows the 1980s way of diving—it's completely different now. They've got a new technique for starting dives.

I was amazed when I saw the Danish version, which I'm told is titled *Andy's Tears.* Some say the cover looks like soft porn. It's a very lovely young girl on the cover. But that certainly is not an athlete's body. Certainly not a swimmer's, because swimmers are, as we all know, quite notably strong in the upper body. I've yet to see a swimmer with breasts like that. I've been told this is a very prestigious publisher and I am delighted it's in Danish at all.

The Afrikaans version was published by Oxford University Press in Capetown. That cover is also anachronistic. I think if Alex wore bathing togs with the very high cut leg like that in 1959, she would have been asked to leave the pool or possibly been arrested. I'm told the South African translation is an extremely good one. The title translates to something about swimming upstream or against the current.

When I give my publisher international rights, I give them rights to arrange translations and send it on to other publishers. Although text is quite obviously copyrighted, titles are not, so foreign publishers are free to choose their own. Of course, I have no say on foreign covers, either.

I have to say the success of *Alex* in New Zealand and internationally has astonished me. It's become a kind of cult here in New Zealand. I trained as a journalist and think I can be fairly objective about my own books. Now these are facts—which obviously give me great pleasure to tell you. Nevertheless, I will try to make it as objective as I can.

The hardback edition of *Alex* was published at the end of 1987. By that time I was already helping to write a film script. Now we are talking about a sequel to the film. Also I'm talking with a young playwright who wants to make a play out of the third Alex book.

Since 1987, *Alex* has been reprinted here three times. The Puffin version has become Penguin New Zealand's biggest selling book of all times. It has sold 23,000 copies. Many of these books have been sold to schools. The quartet has become a standard text in many schools here.

I think my book and Alan Duff's are the only books that have sold in excess of 20,000 copies. That may seem like a small number to you, but in New Zealand terms that's a lot.

Alan Duff's book *Once Were Warriors* has sold something like 25,000 copies. His book is a very important one for us at the moment, and it continues to sell in large numbers. If you take home any single adult novel from here, I recommend this one, which has achieved an astounding success in the last year or so. It addresses the problems of such racial tensions as we have. They are not huge, but they exist.

I will mention a bit about the film of *Alex*, because that's very much on my mind. In April and May the film was shot here in Auckland. At the moment, it is being edited in Sydney.

The film has been a five-year process that seemed to go on and on. A script was written. A script was shelved. Then started again. We went through that process three times.

In 1988 I sat in the office of the director of Television New Zealand and heard the magic words, "We want to make a film out of your book." They were going to make a miniseries at that point. Two years later they had a script for a three-part miniseries and we had funding. Then they closed the drama department and my project, along with quite a few others, was shelved.

After about a year, it was picked up by Isambard, a private production company, which worked with an Australian co-producer. This means the Australian input was

the director, several of the main actors and about half of the
$2 million budget.

One of New Zealand's most successful television screen
writers wrote the script last year. I had quite a lot of input
into it. I think in five years I've learned a lot about television
and films and about script writing. I recognize the
imperatives of working in that medium.

There are changes from the book, which were necessary.
I'm pragmatic about this. Most of the changes, in fact, I'd
say 90 percent of them, I was quite happy with.

I was just talking with the producer this morning about
the plans they have to market the film in New Zealand and
Australia. They're planning a campaign to market it
particularly through the schools in November. By
December, they will have built up an audience, which we
hope will then come in droves. We have our long summer
vacation from mid-November through January. So hopefully
the film will be shown during that period.

Of course, after it's been shown in the cinema, it will be
sold on video. We're all hoping that it will achieve general
release in America, as well. If it doesn't achieve general
release, it almost certainly will be a television movie. The
script was made with that very much in mind. With any
luck, maybe you'll see it next year.

I saw quite a lot of the shooting, which was a very
interesting exercise. Seeing my character come to life in front
of me was an extraordinary experience. They found a young
woman to play the part of Alex who was 5 foot 10 inches
tall, had been to acting school, played the piano very
competently, had done 10 years of ballet, plays hockey, was
very bright at school and her swimming was adequate. In
other words, she was an Alex.

The producers told me they were overwhelmed when
they first called for applicants for this role. When they
advertised that auditions were being held, they had
something like 300 initially. They ruled it down to six, and I
saw those last six audition tapes. The producer was
absolutely amazed at the talents of the kids who auditioned.
They all related to the character and badly wanted to play
her.

Nobody wanted to play Alex more badly than the girl who was chosen. Her name is Lauren Jackson and she's an Alex through and through.

I know because I watched that young woman at 3 o'clock in the morning when they were doing a night shoot. She did a scene where she had to do, first of all, a perfect pirouette. They shot this particular scene three times and every time, at 3 o'clock in the morning, she got it spot on. A beautiful, balanced pirouette. Any of you, who are familiar with ballet, will know a perfect pirouette is one of the most tricky maneuvers in ballet.

Half an hour later, she was having to get up and sing a song from *The Mikado*. She did that perfectly as well. She'd never actually sung in public before, but she was required to do this for the role.

I watched her in every one of the 86 scenes that she appears in this film. Time and time again, I thought, "Well, they have chosen the right girl."

She is not actually a great beauty, but she has a wonderfully transparent face and is a very fine looking young woman. When I say she's not a great beauty, I don't mean to demean her. What I mean is that she doesn't look like the conventional 15-year-old film star. I think she has a much more vibrant and interesting face. I was delighted with the girl they'd chosen.

That's all very exciting because it's prompting the publishers to bring out an Alex omnibus. My publisher in Auckland said the other day, because of the film they're publishing all four books in one volume later this year. It will have 800 pages and the cover will feature a picture of the actress who plays Alex in the film. That's quite exciting to think the whole lot are going to be published in one go.

We have a wonderful scheme here called the New Zealand Writers in Schools. It is run with government money and run very efficiently for one thing. It enables writers to go into schools as invited guests. The schools initiate visits and the scheme pays us a modest fee and expenses.

We go very much on the basis that we are practicing members of a vital artistic community, not as celebrities. I might have had a certain amount of success with my books, but I'm not a celebrity. To the students, I'm a person who's not very different from their own mothers. Sometimes I get the impression that the kids are actually quite disappointed when someone walks in who does actually look like the mothers of all their friends.

I think teachers see us as people who are both colleagues and allies in this business of getting children to love books from the age of three or four onward.

Most of my visits are to high schools. I have to say it's an enormous pleasure for me as a writer, and particularly as a writer of a book seen as having a strong female protagonist dealing with girls' problems, women's problems.

I was strongly influenced by Betty Friedan, writer of that wonderful book *The Feminine Mystique.* When I first read her book, it absolutely opened my eyes. I don't think I read it until 1975, which was quite a long time—13 or 14 years—after she wrote it. I think her book grew out of the general philosophy of the sexes as we saw them and the role of women as we saw it in the 1950s, when Alex and I were growing up. I've tried to reflect this in *Alex.*

What intrigues me is how children these days relate to the situations, because in some way the problems are still there. They may be in a little different form, but they haven't gone away.

I decided to set the quartet in that period right around 1960, partly because those were my own teenage years. I also wanted to set it just before television came to this country and changed our lives dramatically. It came here quite suddenly in 1961 and I would say most people had a black and white set of some sort, probably by 1965. So I set this book quite deliberately at the closing of an era in 1959, when there was no television.

I know you had television in America much earlier. I wonder whether it changed your lives as dramatically when it came in. Or was it a slower process?

I'm very lucky that I started my career as a writer at the beginning of what is now seen as an explosion of children's writing in New Zealand. It started round about 1980. Up to that point we'd had a small number of books—maybe 25 picture books and novels—published every year. Of course, that is very small by your standards.

Up to that point, very few New Zealand writers had been published internationally or been picked up for British or American or Australian co-editions.

I don't believe anyone, with the exception of Margaret Mahy, was published internationally. She, of course, is in a different category from the rest of us. She has been a mentor to many of us. We all revere her immensely, both for her talent and for her generosity to those of us who have come along in her footsteps. She's a wonderful friend and a very funny person.

She has probably created the climate in America and Britain, but particularly in America, where people like me come along, say five years behind her, and find our books have been accepted for co-editions.

Now I'm one of about 30 professional writers in New Zealand writing specifically for children. We are achieving quite significant sales in New Zealand. This is new here. We're only three million people. We have a very small market. We're very good book buyers. Nevertheless, it's a small market.

I have to say, as a group, we're probably one of the strongest groups of writers in our country. The reason we are able to survive professionally is that quite a number of us are being published and achieving quite good sales overseas.

In the young adult area there would be Sherryl Jordan, who is published by Scholastic in New York. Her best-known book is called *Rocco*. She also has a wonderful book called *The Juniper Game*. Joy Cowley is one of our finest writers for both adults and children. Her book *Bow Down, Shadrach* won the Children's Book of the Year award and has been published internationally this year.

William Taylor is another writer you may know. He's published quite widely in the states. Some of his books are *Paradise Lane* and *The Worst Soccer Team Ever,* which was the first in a series about a soccer team which has both boys and girls playing. That one was actually made into a miniseries.

Gaelyn Gordon has received wonderful reviews in the States for her book called *Duckat.* It's a very funny book about a duck who thinks he's a cat. In other words, it's a story about an identity crisis.

Gavin Bishop is a New Zealand author-illustrator recently chosen as one of the world's top 29 illustrators by an authority at the Ohio State University .

Martin Baynton is an author-illustrator whose books *Daniel's Dinosaur* and the *Fifty* series (about a tractor called Fifty) have done very well in the States. He has also published in England.

Lynley Dodd is a very successful writer-illustrator, whose Hairy McLairy books are quite popular internationally. They look so simple, but there's a lot of redrafting, rewriting and reworking. I believe six months hard work goes into every single one of them. She has won the AIM Children's Picture Book of the Year award.

POSTSCRIPT

Since July 1992 when this talk was recorded in Auckland, my life has been an extraordinary mixture of success and tragedy.

In April 1993 *Songs for Alex* was judged the New Zealand Book of the Year in the senior fiction section and also shortlisted for the New Zealand Libraries Association Esther Glen medal. The movie *Alex* had its world premiere in Auckland in May 1993 and has been sold for screening in Italy, Germany, Canada and Britain, though not yet, alas, to the USA. We are still talking about a sequel. I've written and appeared in two plays, and I am working on a third collaboration with the talented writer-illustrator Martin Baynton. I've started another novel for children and have won a major Arts Council fellowship to tour Australia for a month in August-September. I have two books being published this year: for Penguin Books, *Nearly Seventeen,* an anthology of stories for young women, and for Ashton Scholastic, *The Making of Alex: The Movie.*

In July last year, nine days after this talk was given, my 24-year-old daughter Alexandra Clare died in her sleep, suddenly, of a heart condition. She had almost completed six years of study at Auckland University for her Master of Arts and Master of Law degrees. She contributed her energy, vitality, self-discipline, ambition and sense of fun to the character of *Alex* and we dedicated the film to her memory.

GAVIN BISHOP

Gavin Bishop, an author, illustrator and art teacher, describes his books as firmly set in New Zealand with landscapes and buildings representing Christchurch and the surrounding area. He mentions that although those illustrations give the books a strong flavor of the country they come from, dealing with such obvious New Zealand settings may limit book sales. Mr. Bishop's maternal grandfather was Maori, and he brings that influence into some of his books. He's written television scripts and written and designed sets for two ballets for the Royal New Zealand Ballet. A roaring fire in his stone fireplace warmed his living room, when we visited his home in the Cashmere Hills above Christchurch.

I thought I might talk to you about some of the things I've done over the past 14 or so years. I'm very flattered to think that you know anything about my work at all, because I've had some stuff sort of sporadically published in the United States. Hopefully that will change soon because I've been taken under the wing of a studio in Boston called the Studio Goodwin-Sturges.

Some of you may have heard of Judy Sue Goodwin-Sturges, who is a lecturer at the Rhode Island School of Design. She saw my work some years ago and wrote to me to ask if I would care to send her some work so she could represent me in the States. Of course I didn't think about it that long. I quickly sent some off to her.

She's at the moment, I think, in New York taking some of my pictures to some publishing houses. She has some stories sorted out that she wants me to illustrate and hopefully she's going to find a publishing house interested in my work.

I would do the illustrations, but the stories won't be mine. I've seen the stories and I like them—they're funny stories. So you might see more of my stuff in the United States in the future.

The Lion and the Jackal is my only truly American book. It was written by Beverly Dietz and published by

51

Silver-Burdett and Ginn. That was a book I did through
Studio Goodwin-Sturges in Boston.

My most recent project is another where I illustrated
someone else's work. It is called *Little Red Rocking Hood.* I
blanched when I heard the name—I didn't like it. But then
they sent me a tape of the music and when I heard it, I loved
it. It's very funny, very witty.

Little Red Rocking Hood is part of a package for an older
age group that includes a small paperback and a great big
paperback and a tape. It is part of the Australian school
music syllabus. I researched the 1950s so I could use
furniture design and colors from the decade when rock was
first introduced. I thoroughly enjoyed working on it.

I've had work published mainly in New Zealand but also
in England, Australia, Canada and the United States—all
English-speaking places. Recently, my first foreign language
edition was published. *The Three Little Pigs* has gone into
French for a French-Canadian edition. I have sent material to
Japan from time to time. However, no publisher has taken
any up yet.

The Three Little Pigs has been selling quite well in
North America and yet it's quite ironic because the
landscapes in this book to me are very much set in New
Zealand and have a very Canterbury look. American
publishers on the whole seem to be very cautious about this
sort of thing.

Three or four years ago when I was actually working on
this book there was a very bad drought. We usually only get
24 inches of rainfall per year, but this year it didn't rain all
summer.

Farmers all around here were in a predicament. There
was no feed for the stock. The landscape just turned the
color of straw. You could drive through the whole place and
there was practically no grass left. The soil was dry and bits
of straw were blowing around. Then contrasting with that
were shelter-belts of very dark green macrocarpa trees.

That's a main feature of this book. The landscapes in the
backgrounds of the pictures are just like Canterbury in the
summertime. Yet this book has done quite well outside New
Zealand. Somebody told me once that *Mrs. McGinty and the*

Bizarre Plant did well in Kansas because Kansans could relate to the landscape.

I go out quite often to schools to speak to children. I find children always ask the same questions. One is "How much money do you make?" The next question is "How old were you when you first started writing?" quickly followed by "How long ago WAS that?" Finally, they ask "Where do you get your ideas from?"

That's the one I'm going to talk about tonight. I used to say I didn't know really, because they just sort of came. Then I suddenly realized, of course, they come from all around me, from my own environment, people I know, things that I do every day, movies that I watch, and books that I read.

In 1986, a couple of months after *Mother Hubbard* was published, the editor came down to see me. It was the first time she had been to this house. When she came to the door, she said, "Goodness gracious, it's Mother Hubbard's house."

She came inside, and, sure enough, the atmosphere and all the rubbish and things looked just like the house in *Mother Hubbard*. So I sort of unwittingly just used the stuff from around here.

One thing I've always tried to do is to use what I know and what I see around me. I use my own environment. I never tried to be an English picture book artist or an American picture book artist. I take pride in being a New Zealander and in being a New Zealand picture book artist. And I include details that, first of all, children in New Zealand recognize and relate to.

Another thing I've done quite consciously is to use details of Christchurch. The very first book I ever had published—although certainly not the first book I wrote— was called *Mrs. McGinty and the Bizarre Plant.* This was published in 1981. It was very firmly set in a part of Christchurch called Linwood where I used to teach in high school.

The house of Mrs. McGinty, the old lady featured in the book, is actually a real house in Linwood. One day when I was at a school nearby, Linwood Primary School, a little boy raised his hand and said "Excuse me. Do you realize

Mrs. McGinty lives in my aunty's house?" So it's really quite nice to have these little touchstones that the kids can recognize.

One of the famous landmarks in Linwood that appeared in *Mrs. McGinty and the Bizarre Plant* was the Edmund's baking powder factory. It had a big sign above it which said "Sure To Rise" with a big sunburst on the top of it—a beautiful art deco design. Now it's been pulled down. However, it has been featured in my book, and it lives on there.

Without really planning to, I've preserved other old buildings in Christchurch, too.

Just down from the Cashmere area in Christchurch, there used to be a great big, sooty gas works where they burned coal to make gas. That went out of fashion when they realized we had a tremendously huge smog problem and one of the contributors was the gas works, so they tore the gas works down.

I just happened to draw it and include it in my book *Mr. Fox*. I didn't know the place was going to be pulled down, but a year or so after the book came out the gas works that actually appears in those pictures disappeared.

Another building which appears in *Mr. Fox* is the Aulesbrooks factory. That too was pulled down a year or so after it appeared in the book.

The Horror of Hickory Bay is a book which is very dear to my heart, but it hasn't done very well financially. I think it hasn't done well because children don't have a lot to say about what they read. Here, adults have quite a lot to say, and librarians and parents haven't chosen to buy this book. However, I get more letters from children about *The Horror of Hickory Bay* than any of my other books.

The Horror of Hickory Bay was a bit of a challenge. It has only 73 words in it. Sometimes you have whole pages go by where you don't have any words at all. I like wordless books. I would also like to do picture books for older children, but there doesn't seem to be a big market for them.

The Horror of Hickory Bay is about a land form that comes to life and becomes a monster that starts to eat up the things around him, the fish in the sea, the birds in the air, the trees in the forest and so on. The hero is a little girl who is a violinist, and she has a dog called Smudge and a ventriloquist dummy, who plays the harmonica, as a friend. The three of them make a sort of a rumpus and drive the monster back to sea.

I'm quite fond of having females as heroes, probably because I have three daughters of my own. When I wrote this book, my youngest daughter was three or four, and she had decided to learn to play violin. She had just started and she was not very good. Actually, then she was really pretty terrible. She still plays the violin, and now she is quite good. That was one of the things from my family that I used in this book.

Besides my immediate environment, a lot of the things I use are from my childhood. The more I look back into my childhood the more details I remember. Now I'm not sure whether these things really happened or whether I am just imagining them.

When I was two years old, living in Invercargill with my parents and my grandmother, I ran away from home. I wasn't really disgruntled with my life or anything. I ran away because I wanted to visit the birds in an aviary in a park nearby.

I used to go there quite often when I was little. I really can remember quite clearly being pushed in my push-chair up to the wire to see those birds.

This particular day when I ran away from home, I was found and taken back not long after. When I got home my grandmother took me to one side and said, "If you run away again, the beast at the dairy will catch you."

The next day when I was at the corner dairy, which I suppose was like an American drug store, I saw a bulldog. I realized that was what my grandmother had meant when she mentioned the beast at the dairy. That did the trick. I didn't run away from home again.

Forty years later the Royal New Zealand Ballet Company asked me to write a children's story for a ballet set in New Zealand with a distinctive New Zealand flavor, and I ended up using that memory.

I really wracked my brains because I didn't know quite what to do. Then I remembered back to that time when I was two and thought of my running away, and I based the story on that. I called it *Terrible Tom*.

Although I wrote it as very much a fantasy, it was very, very firmly set in Invercargill in my grandmother's little house. And the boy was me, but I made the character, Tom, much older in the ballet.

I was responsible for the design of the ballet, as well as the story. The pictures, which I drew for the costume and set designs, were shown in an exhibition here recently.

Terrible Tom was choreographed by Russell Kerr of the Southern Ballet Company here in Christchurch, and it had brilliant original music as well. It toured throughout New Zealand for 18 months and was featured at the Wellington Arts Festival.

It was popular enough for the Royal New Zealand Ballet to decide to commission a second ballet the following year. So I wrote another one called *Te Maia and the Sea Devil*, which is a legend set on the west coast of the South Island.

The main character is a young Maori girl named *Te Maia*, which means brave and strong. She manages to go beneath the sea and, in fact, rescues her parents who are being held captive there. It is terribly exciting and also very funny. There are dancing sea gulls and dancing crabs with big flippers. Very charming. Lovely ballet.

Another source of ideas is my own family background. I saw some of you coming in from the bus with my book *Katarina*. "Katarina" was the Maori name for my great aunt, Katherine. She and my grandfather were born on the Waikato River in the North Island about an hour's drive south from Auckland.

They were educated by an early English missionary, who set up a mission school and took in Maori children and turned them into Pakeha, white people. The missionaries taught them how to read and write and play piano. They made the children learn all kinds of useless information— like the major tributaries of the Danube. The missionaries really in effect tried to stamp out any traces of their own Maori culture.

The story of Katarina tells of my great aunt who at the age of 18 left her family in the North Island and went south to Fortrose near Invercargill. She produced a family of 12, and she brought up lots of other people's children as well.

Later, my grandfather went down south and joined her. Katarina and my grandfather were the only two from a family of 12 to move south. All the other members of the family stayed in their original tribal area.

My grandfather and great aunt lost contact with the rest of the family. In fact, when recently I met elderly cousins of mine for the first time, they didn't believe, for a start, that I was any relation. They claimed grandfather died without issue at the age of 22.

He married late, at age 46, and had five children. The youngest child was my mother, who was born when he was 70. So I never met him. That would have been slightly impossible. He was actually born in the 1840s. That puts his generation back a long way.

We knew my grandfather was Maori, and he spoke the Maori language fluently much of the time. We knew also he came from the Waikato region on the North Island, but we didn't know what tribe or what specific area.

My brother does lectures in education and Maori studies at Otago University, so he has had the opportunity and the funding to do quite a lot of research. Over the past 10 years or so, he and I have done a lot of investigation into our family history. The things we found make a very moving story. I could speak for hours about my book *Katarina*. It is amazing the repercussions I have had from that book.

It is not an historical piece; it is a work of fiction based on history. The things that happened really did happen, but not necessarily exactly at the time that they do in the story. I thought it was my job, as a writer, to make a good story first.

In the future I would like to do more work like this, working in response to my family background and to other things I'm well acquainted with.

In the past five or 10 years, there's been tremendous resurgence of interest in New Zealand about the Maori. People have realized what a valuable thing this is and want to foster this knowledge. The Maori language is being revived and being taught not only in state schools, but also in bilingual schools.

Over the summer, I'm going to work on another book with a Maori theme. Hinepau was my mother's name and also my great-grandmother's. It's a very old name on the east coast of North Island. Hinepau is the heroine in this story about a woman victimized by her tribe, but who in the end is the one who saves the day. It's really a kind of a legend I've made up.

Some Maori people don't think it's right to make up this kind of story, but I feel this is my family, my ancestry—I can use it if I want to as long as I treat it with respect.

In this book there are a few very basic Maori words—ones I would say every New Zealander should know. Primary teachers now are being taught Maori, so they have some familiarity with the language.

It is very unlikely that a book with a Maori theme would be published any place else except in New Zealand. If it were published overseas, it would need a glossary, some explanation of the words. I don't want a glossary in that book when it is published here. If you include a glossary, in a way it's like an apology for using those words. I want to use Maori words in a way that will help people move toward understanding them.

My book *Mr. Fox* is set in New Zealand, although no foxes are found here. I tend to think certain sorts of animals and characters are universal. It's an interesting story, and I used to read it to my children over and over when they were little.

When I decided to turn it into a picture book, I wrote to my wife's cousin who works in New Jersey. She was a librarian at the time, and I asked her to find out how old that story was and to see if she could find a really early version of it through her computer.

She wrote back and said the best she could find was an early version of a Massachusetts chain story. Some people think the story of Mr. Fox is probably pre-Elizabethan and very, very old. I think it probably went across to the eastern United States with the Pilgrims.

Since it's a very old story, I thought it would work in New Zealand. I didn't want to change it, but the original story may have been quite racist, referring to people by color, such as yellow and black. I sidestepped that issue and turned colors into other things such as reference to occupations or hobbies.

Several of my books have been based on old folktales. Where possible, when I rework a folktale like *Chicken Licken* or the *Three Little Pigs,* I go to the oldest source I can possibly find, because I always find the oldest versions are the gutsiest, the richest in detail. They don't beat around the bush and you get the real story. Besides those early folk tales were not really meant for children—they were meant for everyone.

The trouble is that folktales have been taken through a kind of Walt Disney process this century. Walt Disney has his three pigs all dancing and skipping on down the road at the end, which completely defeats the purpose of the whole story.

It's just like *Chicken Licken* where the other birds have to be eaten to make any sense of the story. The modern versions completely disregard the moral. I don't like beating around the bush the way the modern versions do.

I've had very little flak about using the old versions of folktales. I think people take them for what they are. Certainly I've read many, many, many folktales to children and have never had a child break down.

Another book I'd like to talk about is *BidiBidi.* This book belongs to New Zealand. It belongs to this part of the world, to Canterbury and the high country, and places like Mt. Cook and the Southern Alps of the South Island. Anyone who has been to New Zealand will recognize the landscapes in this book.

When I first started to write for children, this is the book I started off with. I started writing it in 1978, and it wasn't published until 1982. But it's never been out of print here and it's been the basis for two television series. It's a constantly popular book.

This is the story that goes behind the scenes. I first started writing *BidiBidi* because I wanted to write a New Zealand children's book, a book that really was like New Zealand. I'm sure that's the reason for its success here. That's also been the reason for its lack of success anywhere else. In fact, it's only ever been published here and in Australia.

The American branch of Oxford University Press was quite interested in publishing it at one time, but on second thought, they decided it was too strange, too foreign. We got the same answer from everywhere else.

When I first started writing it, I knew absolutely nothing about writing children's books. I didn't know how long the text should be. I didn't know where the pictures should come. I really had no idea. So I started writing the story and about 4,000 words later I realized I should be coming to some sort of conclusion. So I wound it up and I started doing some pictures and then I thought "I'm not quite sure what I'm doing."

So I bundled it all up and sent it off to Oxford University Press. They didn't accept right off. They said it was very rough, and it needed quite a lot of work. But they were interested and they would work on it with me, because they would certainly like to publish it at some stage.

That's when the work started. I worked on this book with two editors. First of all Brigit Williams, who now has her own publishing house, worked on it with me for several months. Then Wendy Harrex took over. She and I worked on it for months and months. And she kept encouraging me to reduce the text. I would chop out great chunks of it and then rewrite the whole thing and send it off to her in Auckland. She would write back and say, "Yes, it's much better, but it is still too long—keep going."

So I'd keep on chopping more and more of the text. Originally, it was full of poems and songs. It was everything I'd ever wanted to have in a children's book.

She kept saying, "I like the story, but I'm not too sure about some of those poems."

And so I would work on them and try to improve them. I thought it might be a good idea to write some as haiku. After I sent them off to Wendy, she replied, "Yes, they are better and they might appeal to the Japanese market." Later though, the whole section with the haiku disappeared with further editing.

I took a tremendous amount of care in drawing the plants and animals and birds to be sure they were quite accurate and true to location and also the time of the year when the story takes place. I wanted to be sure which plants would actually be flowering there in the high country in the summertime. Although I can see now where I could rewrite and do some things better, this is a book I'm really proud of.

While I was doing my research, I caught the name of BidiBidi. BidiBidi is a small plant, prickly with seed heads with little hooks that catch onto the wool of sheep or onto your socks. I believe the early Europeans boiled BidiBidi and made tea out of it. BidiBidi is the English version of the Maori word PiriPiri. That's where the word BidiBidi came from.

At one stage when there didn't seem any likelihood the book would be published because of financial reasons, Wendy Harrex approached the New Zealand wool board and asked if they would be interested in subsidizing a children's book. They said no because they didn't think the word BidiBidi or the idea of a burr like BidiBidi would have a very positive image for the wool industry.

Finally, because of a lack of foreign support, it didn't seem there was any likelihood of the book being published here. The only reason it was published in the end was that I said I would accept half royalties for the book. So the publisher said, "We'll publish it on the understanding that you receive half the royalties on the first 3,000 books." Well, the first 3,000 copies were actually sold in about two months. So then my royalties went on to 10 percent.

New Zealand book stores don't hold a lot of stock of any one book. Since we can really safely expect to sell only about 3,000 copies of a book here, most New Zealanders need foreign support for their publishing. They extend their print run by getting foreign publishers to buy in.

I think publishers are more conservative than their readers about books with a strong sense of place. I know that in New Zealand we have always been delighted to get a book with the strong flavor of the country it comes from. I think it's sad we're being expected to homogenize everything with books that could go anywhere and fit anything. If you read a book that could be set anyplace, I think a special quality is lost.

I blundered my way through *BidiBidi*. I'm much wiser now, and I've found a lot more shortcuts. One thing that I do now is to make up a dummy. But I didn't know about dummies when I started. An Australian children's author called Ron Brooks taught me how to use them.

For those of you who don't know, a dummy is a blank book the same shape and size and with the same number of pages the final book is going to have. Then you simply go through and work in pencil to rough out and move things around. I rub things out and change things around. Some primary teachers don't like the idea because they don't like kids rubbing things out.

Then I write the text in so I can see how the text will fit and I write myself little notes. When I'm finished, I show it to my editor, and she can see what I have in mind. The dummy gives us something concrete to discuss. By the time I come to the final artwork, all I have to do is to trace the drawings and transfer them to watercolor paper and do them in full color.

All the original art work from *Mr. Fox* has been on exhibition in the city art gallery. They're holding on to the art at the moment, deciding whether to send the exhibition around New Zealand as a traveling show or not.

My later dummies are much rougher and I do them much more quickly. I draw in a sort of shorthand now. Wendy Harrex and I have been working together for so long; she sort of knows what I've got in mind anyway. She'll reject or accept my ideas based on the dummy. She can be quite hard.

When she comes up with an idea and asks for a change, she usually has a pretty good reason. When she tells me to change something, I usually don't mind. I've been very grateful at times for her to return a drawing to me with a comment. I'll look at it again and, sure enough, I'll often realize she's right.

I get to a stage where I can't see what I'm doing. I work so closely on a book that after awhile I can't see it, I really can't see it. Wendy looks at it with a fresh viewpoint.

Before I got involved in books, I used to paint and nobody was there to say, I think you should change that or if you changed that, it would be better. Nobody had a vested interest in what I was doing. No one worried either if I were to stop painting.

When working on a book, I have quite a lot of people who are investing a large amount of money. I want my book to be the best product possible. Another thing that scares me is that there are so many thousands of copies, and any mistakes are multiplied thousands and thousands of times.

When I first started I knew absolutely nothing about writing a book, and it scared me. But now I actually quite like it. The pictures never get easier—it's difficult intensive work. I find that my eyes suffer. Sitting so long is a form of torture. (In teaching I'm on the move all the time.) Physically, I suffer from sitting at a table for hours on end. I work in a studio downstairs. Sometimes I work late in the summertime, and at the end of a long day, I feel so sort of crippled I can hardly get up the stairs.

Whenever I start off on a new book, I'm really excited about it. I have to be excited about it, or else I can't do it. When I'm supposed to be starting a project, I put it off for ages. I move things around or go see somebody or something like that to delay starting. Then I sort of play around with rough sketches and perhaps make a few dummies. And I'll play around with the style of type and things like that.

I put off actually starting the drawing, because I know once I start doing the work something else seems to take over. Obviously, some kind of innate ability governs all those things that make you draw the way you do. They come into play and they start to control what you're doing. And you've lost your control over it. It never turns out to be as exciting and as wonderful as you originally had in your mind.

When a book is first printed and I see the first copies, that's a terrible experience. It's not exciting. I go through it and I suddenly see all these things I should have done, but I didn't see at the time. Little things jump out. At first, whenever I looked at my book or even thought about it, I felt sick. Gradually, I would get some distance and be able to look at it objectively.

When the kids ask about how much money I make, I tell them the fact that I still teach full-time at a high school answers that question. Yeah, I do make some money in some sort of spasmodic and unreliable form. Most writers I know in New Zealand don't actually live off income from their books.

If I do a television series, then, of course, the income is quite good. But that's only for one year. Then the following year I might make $2,000 or $3,000. All my early books are out of print—they're no longer stocked in shops. I should imagine that the only way to make a good income is to have 15 or 20 books selling reasonably well at one time. If all the early ones are gradually dying and only the most recent ones are selling, that makes a difference.

You do get some nice spin-offs writing for children. I get letters from all over the place. I just got one from a child in Texas, writing to say he liked *Three Little Pigs*. It's actually very, very nice. Those little bits of feedback are very exciting.

Those little things that I don't know are going to happen are better than money. Suddenly the phone will ring and they'll say "Will you come and speak?" In September I'm going to give lectures in China with UNESCO.

I actually teach art in a boys' school and right now teach boys who have been brought up on *Mrs. McGinty* and *BidiBidi* and some of my other books. Those books are part of their childhood and that delights me. A lot of them realize I wrote those books, but a lot of them don't. And I've had funny conversations with boys who have said to me, "Oh I remember a book about this old lady, Mrs. McGinty. Do you know that one?"

And I'll say, "Well, actually I wrote it." Sometimes they think I'm just having them on. I like to think some part of my kids' books will be part of them for the rest of their lives.

MARGARET MAHY

Margaret Mahy is the foremost author of children's and young adult literature in New Zealand. She has won major awards in Britain, the United States, and New Zealand. Betty Gilderdale has written a book about Margaret Mahy for children that answers questions they frequently ask about one of their favorite authors. As she told us about the influences that shaped her as a writer, we learned a lot about the evolution of children's literature in New Zealand, as well. She invited us to her townhouse in Christchurch, the most English town outside the United Kingdom. The townhouse is in the shell of a typically British stone building, which originally housed a girls' school. The building was condemned because it wasn't earthquake proof. Preservationists effected a compromise. The classic building was gutted, then reinforced and turned into townhouses.

Recently I saw yet again the film version of *The Wizard of Oz* starring Judy Garland, and was struck with the scene where Dorothy, the Scarecrow and The Tin Man come into one of those mysterious forests, which crop up in so many fairy stories. As they go in they say in an increasingly rhythmic chorus, "Lions and tigers and bears—Oh my! Lions and tigers and bears—Oh my!" And it occurred to me that, if I had to give a title to this talk, this would be a particularly suitable one, not only because I feel a little as if I too am entering that mysterious forest myself.

I am going to talk to you today about the impact that stories and reading had on me when I was a child—an impact so powerful that it determined the form that my life would take, the work I chose to do, and determines to this day some of the ways I react to things that happen to me. It may be that I was particularly vulnerable, but I believe that all children respond to stories and that stories help them find their place in the world.

The earliest stories I can remember hearing come from 1939, the year I was three years old, and I can't truly remember the first one which was a story my father made up for me. Indeed, I remember only its first line, "Once upon a

time there was a great big black-maned Abyssinian lion…" It
is only the spell of its announcement that I remember,
because the story changed from one telling to the next.
However, the opening remained the same and was repeated
many times which is no doubt why I remember it still. The
second was a story originally published by the Algonquin
Publishing Company and written by Dixie Wilson and
entitled *The Honey Bear*. I have to admit that I was not so
precocious as to record either publisher or author when I
was three years old. I only know these details because I still
have the book. It was given to me when I was three years
old and was unusual in that it came from the USA. Nearly all
the books available in New Zealand at that time came from
Great Britain.

It is my intention to gossip a little about the complicated
nature of stories from the point of view of an individual New
Zealander whose childhood was marked by happy collisions
of family told stories and their more cultured literary
relations—good books, and at the same time disjointed by a
post-colonial experience common to many New Zealanders
of my age, that of living under the Southern Cross in a
family which looked back to Europe and particularly to
England for stories to furnish and indeed establish our
imaginations—for intimations of what sort of world it was,
what we should hope for in it, what sort of lives we should
try to lead in it, and who were we anyway, we, the tongues
that were telling the stories, the ears that were listening.

As you probably know, New Zealand is one of many
countries thrown out of true by vast distortions of
colonialism. Indeed, I think we have some common ground
with the USA in this, though colonialism is more of a distant
presence in the USA, which now has a national personality
so well developed that it can be recognized in any part of the
world. In fact this personality colonizes other countries,
mainly through advertising, films and music.

Anyhow, in the beginning my own imagination was not
a New Zealand one, but was populated with fairies, elves
and giants, with talking animals, cunning foxes, tigers,
noble lions, grumbling bears and rabbits in blue coats. It
celebrated a Christmas of English robins and holly and bare
branches against snow or a winter sky—this is a country

with no native mammals—a country of birds who live in or under trees that are never bare. All the same though I notice the disjunctions, I cannot regret them, because, if the stories I heard in my childhood disinherited me locally to some extent, they nevertheless tied me into a much bigger network. To some extent, they made me, imaginatively, a world citizen. They are one of the reasons I am speaking to you today.

The British influence is certainly not one I am going to reject. It was very important to me, and it still is. I was one of a generation of New Zealanders who went through this imaginative dislocation because the books I read were so predominately British, and I was encouraged, by this influence, to think that my own country had very little to offer—that we New Zealanders were not part of the imaginative content of the world.

New Zealand writing and publishing for children has a long history, but it is also thin and intermittent. Not many of the books that were published were competently marketed. Some writers, like the writer from the 1920s Isobel Maude Peacock, were powerfully influenced by English models themselves, so that, even though they set their books in New Zealand, a sort of "Englishness" filtered through, reinforcing the impact of the mass of English titles. Still, books were published in New Zealand and kept on appearing even if the numbers were small. In 1936, the year I was born, Betty Gilderdale, in her book *A Sea Change* lists five titles published for children. Distribution was difficult,—it still is— and locally published books were often not easily available if you lived, as I did, in a country town.

I began to write children's books consciously when I was about 19 or 20, and I began what I regard as my public writing career when I was 25 and began to have stories published in the *New Zealand School Journal.*

This journal has been published for over 80 years and has been innovative and even challenging in its time. I was delighted to have stories appearing in it, but when I tried to step beyond the *School Journal* and submitted manuscripts to local or Australian publishers, I was regularly told that my stories were "too English" and would be competing with books that came into the country from overseas. What was being looked for by the publishers in New Zealand were stories that featured New Zealand. The reasons for this were practical ones—the New Zealand publisher of the time was competing with businesses overseas who could do big print runs and price books more cheaply. The one advantage that a New Zealand publisher could offer during the 1960s was a book which featured his or her own country, for at long last some rumor that we had our own identity was beginning to circulate at a reasonably popular level. However, when I tried to write stories that featured New Zealand, I found I could not do it with grace or ease. I was the inhabitant of *Elsewhere*, a country with no name, no dimensions, but inhabited by a certain kind of character and event, initially owing its prevalent cast to British writers like Eleanor Farjeon and Walter de la Mare. When I tried to feature my own country, it shrank from me or decked itself out in stiff canvas and plywood. I myself did not believe what I had written.

Then I had one of those wonderful pieces of good luck that one is never encouraged to hope for when you are a writer. The *New Zealand School Journal* containing a story of mine, *A Lion in the Meadow*, was sent to an international publishing exhibition in New York. An editor who worked with the publisher Franklin Watts Inc. wandered into the exhibition, read my story, and thought it would make a good picture book. She wrote to me asking if I would be interested in having the story published as a book, and if it was even available for publication.

I received the letter when I was working at the School Library Service (part of the National Library of New Zealand). I opened it—read it—and felt I was dissolving. The idea of actually having a book published was overwhelming, though it was one that had been with me for many years. Of course in the first few seconds, I knew I was going to write back and say, "Yes, I would love to have the story published as a picture book. Please take it." I was going to be actually published—at last!

A Lion in the Meadow was published in 1969 and brought an amazing personality into my life. Helen Hoke Watts wrote and edited under the name of Helen Hoke, and she was the sort of person who could only be called larger than life—well, a lot larger than my life anyway.

I was living with my two daughters in two rooms that had neither running water nor sewerage. Later we did have water tanks installed and caught rainwater from the roof, but at that time I was carrying water in plastic containers from the library over the hill to my home. I was still digging out the tank stand.

Helen Hoke came to visit me here in New Zealand, coming more or less directly from the Savoy Hotel in London. This woman was about to confer a great blessing on me. She was about to publish my first book. She got off the plane at Christchurch airport and the first words I heard her say were, "My God, this really is the end of the world! They don't recognize American Express."

She was traveling with so much luggage we had to hire two taxis, one to carry the luggage and another in which we sat and talked with reasonable ease as we were carried out of Christchurch to my home in Governor's Bay and the Ocean View Hotel, an establishment which proved to be deficient in the large amounts of ice Helen needed. Nowadays this would be no problem, but in 1969 iced water was a surprising novelty for many New Zealanders.

Helen was to launch my books in the USA with a generosity that I did not appreciate at the time, simply because I did not understand it. I thought it was wonderful, but I didn't altogether realize how unusual it was. Franklin Watts Inc. published not one, but five, picture books together with an elegant colored folder promoting them. It is possible for people to be put off by a commercial hard-sell, and indeed some critics were, but there is no way I can be anything but enormously grateful to Helen for this spectacular introduction. I remember her enthusiasm vividly, and there are other things I remember, too. I remember her saying with strong approval that nobody could tell my books were New Zealand books. I was not upset or insulted. I was too glad to be getting books published. However, it did give me a tremble of self doubt, because, after all, I was a New Zealander and the books were constructed out of what New Zealand had offered me. It offered me the idea that though we were good at producing butter and wool, our own artistic

ideas had no authority—that it was overseas that
Imagination-with-a-capital-"I" flourished most richly, and
that what we did in Auckland or Christchurch was bound to
be inferior in both skill and essence. I shared with other
New Zealanders the feeling that being recognized *overseas*
proved one's excellence. At the same time, as I have already
said, our imaginations are naturally colonized by what comes
at us from the outside world—stories from Britain, music
and images from the United States. Let me go back in time
and say a little more about this.

When I was a child, Western films reigned supreme in
one of our local picture theaters. Roy Rogers, Gene Autry,
Tim Holt—people like these affected my childhood. These
were the people that I wanted to be like. They rode beautiful
horses and had power over life and death. They saved the
good and shot the bad. In those days of clean-shaven
heroes, you could always tell the villain the moment he
appeared on the screen, for he sported a thin little black
mustache. On one never-to-be-forgotten day, I saw outside
the Grand Theater a poster for a film about the female outlaw
Belle Starr. I think Jean or maybe Gene Tierney was the
actress. I don't really remember, and I was not allowed to go
and see the film anyway. Yet the poster was enough—there
she was, a woman dressed as a man, riding a wild horse and
carrying a gun in her hand. It was the most feminist image
the times had to offer me.

I was bewitched by this person. I wanted to *be* her, and
failing that, to write about her. I knew you shouldn't copy
another person's story, and I knew Belle Starr was a real
woman. I altered her for my own purposes. I made her 11
years old—my own age—and I called her Belle Gray. She
was the leader of a gang in the wild west—in Colorado,
because I liked the sound of the name. (Actually, I've
always been rather confused about the West. I thought Texas
was the most western part of the USA. It's only in recent
years I've found out it is actually the south.) Belle Gray was
a persona who dominated my imagination for a year or two.
Once again, she has nothing much to do with New Zealand,
and yet I don't regret her. In some ways she is with me still.

When I'm traveling in Britain, I think of books. When
I'm traveling in the USA, I think of songs. *New York, New*

York or *Chicago, Chicago* or [quaint little villages on] *Old Cape Cod* or *Do You Know the Way to San Jose?* or *Galveston, Oh Galveston.* If ever I visit Galveston there will be words in my head in advance to meet it. Although at times in New Zealand I feel rather apologetic about my imaginative displacement, I have enjoyed it too. I have enjoyed feeling like Kim, in Rudyard Kipling's novel, a citizen of the world.

Most of the trade book publishing I have done has been in the United Kingdom. The first five books Helen Hoke Watts published were co-published in the United Kingdom, and no doubt for reasons I have already indicated, were received there much more enthusiastically than in the USA, in spite of the handsome colored folder. And no wonder, they were in a British style. Perhaps the first book of mine to really do well in the USA did so because of the illustrator. *The Boy Who Was Followed Home* was illustrated by Steven Kellogg. It still remains one of my favorite picture books, partly because I was so pleased with myself for producing a short text, and partly because I think it is a true picture book rather than a story with pictures, and there is a significant difference, but that is the subject of a talk in itself. If *The Boy Who Was Followed Home* is a true picture book, it is because of Steven's approach, not only to illustration, but to the book as a whole.

When I write a story, even though I know it is going to be used as the text for a picture book, my primary concern is with how the story is going to *sound*. Of course I have ideas about the pictures that should accompany the text, but they are somehow fluid. It is often easy for me to adapt to the pictures that an illustrator supplies. However, I do have strong ideas about what the story should be like to *listen* to. *The Boy Who Was Followed Home* was first published in the *New Zealand School Journal*, but in the *School Journal* the story ended in a slightly different way to the way the story in the book ends. In the original story, Robert, having been set free from the attentive hippos, turns around and finds he is being followed by elephants.

In terms of the listening ear, elephants work well. Robert is now being followed by even larger and less controllable animals than the hippos. However, Steven wanted to change the end to make it more of an illustrator's book. He wanted to draw *giraffes* which present a greater pictorial contrast to hippos than do elephants, and he wanted something rather more difficult for an author to agree to—he wanted the words to stop so that the pictures alone could carry the climax of the story. In the event, I agreed to Steven's suggestions with the proviso that there be a final line, so that the story would end for the listener as well as for the person looking at the pictures. In the end there can be a writer's story and an illustrator's story within a single cover, and in *The Boy Who Was Followed Home* Steven has drawn a story of his own that is not reflected in the words.

The reader enters a landscape in which people, hippos, witches, and giraffes mix together, not without difficulties, but quite amiably and naturally on the whole. The school and the child's home are joined by a winding road and a bridge on which two frogs, couchant, smile enigmatically at the comings and goings, the dramas and astonishments that beset the travelers. The school and the house sit in a wide empty country, through which parents drive in long gracious cars that suggest a royal progress of Bentleys and Rolls Royces until they tangle with the proliferating hippos that follow the hero Robert to and from school. It isn't Britain or New Zealand, and it isn't the USA either. It is a country created by stories from childhood, and I still live there to some extent, but I suppose we readers all do, whenever we choose.

I have suggested that I have a primary loyalty to the way a story sounds, and I think the reasons for this lie once again in my childhood. Before I was old enough to write down the stories I wrote as a child, I used to make up poems and stories, and the only way I could retain these brief constructions was to learn them by heart. But then I grew up at a time when many adults also knew things by heart, and I was surrounded by people who seemed able to bring stories and poems out of themselves at need. They knew things by heart because they'd been forced to learn them at school.

I don't know what they thought about being forced to learn poems this way. They probably didn't enjoy it much at the time. However, I am certain that they enjoyed having the stories and poems inside them, easily available when they were adults. They liked being able to recite things for children, and partly for themselves too.

My father knew ballads by W. S. Gilbert and the Australian bush poets "Banjo" Patterson and Henry Lawson. I listened to him recite them, and grew up with the expectation that I too would learn and remember stories in that way. Indeed that is probably why the sound of the story is so important to me, but I say this with no complacency, because I do think the illustrations in books are wonderful. There is no reason why we should not have both told stories and illustrated ones to work in our lives, though they work in different ways.

I do think the outstanding picture books of the world are by people who have both written and illustrated the story, or by people who have worked very closely together. The books by Maurice Sendak, or Harve and Margot Zemach are beautifully integrated, and one cannot detach the story from the pictures or the pictures from the story. They are welded together into an inseparable whole. But of course the sort of book I am involved in—the sort where the story precedes and is supported by the pictures—can be wonderful too, particularly when the writer and artist establish a sympathetic humor, and this can happen even when oceans roll between them.

Every now and then children ask me how I began writing. They often mean when did I start having books published, for unpublished books don't seem altogether real to many children, who need the authority of print to feel a story is authentic. However I point out to them that I began writing when I was seven. My mother saved that first book, a series of pages sewed together, so that tells you something of the sort of family I came from. Years later she gave it back to me, and I have it still. I am able to show the children and point out to them that it does not take very much to begin being a writer—it is an activity accessible to anyone who happens to be interested. What I remember most about this first book is the way I tried hard to make it look as much like a book as possible. I wrote my name in small print at the top of the pages and then the title of the book (*Harry Is Bad*) underneath the author's name and at the conclusion of the story I wrote THE END in big letters, just in case there was

any doubt about it. In those days many books and films
finished with the words THE END. To me it was part of the
form—part of what made the story authentic. Still compelled
by form, I went on to write in notebooks. I thought my
stories had to fit exactly into the notebook covers, for stories
I had read fitted so neatly in between covers supplied by the
publishers. You would never find 20 empty pages at the end
or a note saying that, in order to read the last chapter of the
story you should look in another book. So when I got
halfway through my notebook I knew I was halfway
through my story and I would celebrate by drawing pictures.

Between the ages of eight and eleven, the books I wrote
were almost all about horses. This was partly because I was
so enraptured by the books like Mary O'Hara's *My Friend
Flicka* and *Thunderhead*. I really loved those stories about
beautiful, wild horses which only one magical child (in this
case a boy, Ken McLaughlin) could control. I think these
stories do have something romantic and archetypal about
them, something that carries through into such books as
Pagan the Black, by Dorothy Benedict, or Walter Farley's
book *The Black Stallion*. Certain children, mostly girls,
reproduce these elements in their own stories. A few years
ago I was given a manuscript to read. It consisted of almost
a hundred pages written by a girl of ten, and was quite
impressive in terms of its sophistication as well as its length.
It started off rather in this way. "The girl galloped down the
beach on the beautiful black stallion. Her hair blew out in the
wind behind her." As I read this opening I thought, with
some astonishment, that things had not changed much over
the years, for this seemed to be exactly the underlying idea
of my own first stories.

One of my notebooks contained the story of a beautiful
black stallion, and when I reached the end of the notebook I
wrote *To be continued* for I planned to write other stories
about this paragon of a horse. But I was not always so
inventive. In another notebook, one about a white mare, I
ran out of ideas and tried to make the notebook match my
capacity by cutting pages out of the back to shorten it.
Indeed, I did all those things that children do to increase the
length of a story without going to the trouble of actually
writing it. I stretched out my writing and drew more pictures

than I usually did. Looking at these pictures I realize that I must have had some clear idea of the limits to which my cheating should go. I could have had pictures on every page. I could have had pictures that *filled* a whole page. However, my pictures took up a mere half page though I drew tall trees in the background—pines or poplars—which stretched the picture upwards to what I obviously regarded as a reasonable extent. Neither the stretched-out writing or the tall trees enabled me to finish this particular book, and of course there were many stories back then that were never finished.

I went on writing like this for a long time. I was consistent and I was an opportunist—always on the lookout for the chance to get something into print. Our local paper, *The Bay of Plenty Beacon*, used to feature a children's column every Friday. Anyone who had a poem or story or joke published in this column would receive a certain number of points, and when the writer had gained ten points, he or she received a free ticket to the pictures. So in a way, I have always looked for the chance to write for profit. I still have photocopies of a few of those pages. The date on the one at the top of the pile is Friday, September 7th, 1945.

As well as contributing to this newspaper column whenever possible, I used to go in for competitions in a small monthly magazine called *The Junior Digest,* and every now and then I would enter a competition successfully. I remember opening the issue in which I was first featured in a competition (one in which I came second) and thinking, "This proves it! I really *am* going to be a writer."

In talking about these steps I have taken towards being a writer, I have reversed the order of events, working my way back to my beginnings which were simple and ordinary enough. I was not the only child to write stories. Indeed, I can remember two girls of about my own age who used to write in notebooks and contribute poems to the children's column in the local paper, and as far as I can remember, they were just as good at writing as I was. However, they were less persistent. When we started to attend a secondary school, they stopped writing, and I kept on, which suggests that a big part of a writer's life is sheer obstinacy. At least that seems to be true of me and mine.

I have made my living as a writer for 14 years, writing books used only in schools, trade books and television scripts. But then I swore, when I became a full-time writer, that I would do any work moderately compatible with self-respect. As it happens I am as happy with some of the stories in the whole language reading series as I am with any of the books I have written.

Some of them are very simple books (the shortest is only nine words long) and some are much longer and more complex books for young adults. I have written books for readers who fit somewhere in between three and 16 years of age. Along with books like *Memory* or *Catalogue of the Universe,* I have written nonsense novels like *The Blood and Thunder Adventures on Hurricane Peak* or *The Pirates' Mixed-Up Voyage*, so I am lucky enough to deal with a great variety and to be entertained with nearly everything I do.

Writing can take many forms, and many things are true about it. I think it is best seen, not so much as a single act, but as a series of acts—a flow. Ideas come from outside, often through other books, and inhabit an author for awhile. But in the end, if he or she is a successful writer, the ideas flow on to readers somewhere. Once the connection is made, they become the reader's ideas, and, mysteriously, though different readers may read the same words on identical pages, they use them differently. Some accept the story the words tell eagerly; others reject it.

I believe that the first stories we hear in our families are as close to being tribal stories as you can get without having the benefit of a tribe. They are a sort of instruction which said, "Now listen here—listen to what I am going to tell you—," and involved the surrender of self to the life of the story. The spells that compelled listening were the chosen words. For all the great semiconscious processes that promote our survival—eating and reproduction most notably I suppose—are reinforced with strong pleasure principles and social rituals, and so is the acquisition of language, with all that it brings. I have tried to be the sort of writer that adds to this process; that makes me part of it not only as writer, but as reader too, for my own reading is not finished. I hope to go on reading for many years yet and to continue to grow

through stories, as I have grown through them for many
years.

MARK MacLEOD

Mark MacLeod, Children's Publishing Director, Random House Australia, is a former professor of children's literature in the United States, as well as in Australia. He gave us an overview of Australian culture and children's books. When he mentioned that Australians stereotype Americans as brash and loud and besides that, they have big teeth, we laughed. The New Zealanders had whispered warnings that we would find the Australians brash and loud; although they made no comments about Australian teeth. He spoke to us at the Rozelle Writers' Centre outside Sydney, and we saw him at various functions during Children's Book Week.

I have taught students from Wisconsin and Florida in children's literature, and I have a few observations which may be useful to you. Forgive me if these are stating or restating the obvious. But I think they bear keeping in mind.

One thing is staggering to me: I still don't quite take it in. Australia is, as you know, roughly the same size geographically as the continental United States. But we have 17 million people, compared to 240 million in the United States in roughly the same area of land. Of those 17 million people, nearly half live in two cities—Sydney and Melbourne.

Now that's had a lot of consequences for the kinds of things that you'll find cropping up in Australian literature. When you read early Australian books, and even current Australian books, you'll find that people are quite concerned about the weather. People tell me Australians talk more about the weather than anyone else in the world. I don't know if that's true. But it seems to me there's a lot more landscape and a lot more of nature per head of population here than in the United States. I think that's one of the reasons we talk about it a lot.

You'll notice the differentness of nature in Australia and how this affects the behavior of the people. Early theorists viewed the differentness of the climate and nature and so on as creating different speech linguistically. It's bizarre. But they even said there's so much pollen in the air in Australia, it blocks up the nasal passages and makes us talk very nasally.

Another thing that's really important in the whole understanding of Australian culture is that Australia was one of the last countries to be colonized. Remember, it was colonized at the end of the 18th century when Europe was very much concerned with the industrial revolution and with brand new developments in science and technology. In this country, the settlers came up against one of the world's oldest civilizations. If not the oldest.

People have been forming communities in Australia for 40,000 years. Some say 60,000 years. One Australian says 100,000 years. This is really quite staggering. And it's a theme that runs constant through Australian culture—the meeting of the old and new and, in some sense, the invalidation of both from the old point of view.

To look at the new Australia from an Aboriginal point of view is to kind of think, "Well, you folks are so recently arrived." Many Aboriginal people tell me they have to look at the preoccupation of white Australians with technology, with videos and all that sort of thing, and just kind of laugh privately to themselves.

When non-Aboriginal Australians have recognized the existence and power of the Aboriginal Australian culture, they have looked at it in a kind of complete lack of comprehension. How Aboriginal culture can deal with that much time, that meeting of the old and new, is really important in Australia.

Of course, it's almost a cliché of Australian culture that Australia is at the bottom of the world. Well, it's not quite the last stop on the line. It's the second to last stop. Australians take some comfort from the fact that New Zealand is the true antipodes, at the opposite end of the earth from the United Kingdom. So there is certainly that sense.

And running through the whole early Australian culture is this preoccupation with the strangeness of the culture. It focuses on times like Christmases and birthdays and so on.

Of course, right now in July, in the United States it's hot. Here it's cold—it's winter. At Christmas, you're enjoying Christmas trees in snow, if you live in that part of the United States where that happens. In Australia we're sweltering and kind of panting on the verandah. It is just so hot; it is almost impossible to eat the ridiculous food people eat at Christmas here. So there are very strong elements of irony and contrast in Australian culture.

Australians will have some observations about you, too. First of all, Australians perceive Americans as being powerful and big and loud. One of the commonest experiences of American students in Australia is to have Australians embarrassed by the loudness of their voices. I mean this is really ironic coming from someone like me, I know. But it is very common for Australian students to be walking along the sidewalk and say to an American friend "Shhh." I don't know where this comes from.

If you're into psychology, maybe you understand why the rest of the world perceives Americans as having loud voices. Now I know very well there are many quietly spoken American people. There are many shy American people.

Stereotypes often have nothing to do with the reality of everyday life. But stereotypes are very powerful ideas that kind of float up there above us. And they really govern our behavior.

I don't know whether you will become more American on your tour than you usually are. That would be very interesting. It certainly happens with Australians.

When I'm outside Australia, one of the things I hate the most is when somebody says to me, "Listen there's this Australian I've just met. You must meet him. You will love this person." And within two seconds, I hate this person. We haven't got anything in common. And this person seems to represent everything I hate the most about Australia. It doesn't happen so much to us anymore.

When I first went to the United States, I would notice
while I was talking that people's heads would kind of turn to
one side. I realized in a few sentences that they were not
listening to anything I was saying at all. They were just
listening to the way I was saying it.

Many times in the middle of a really passionate statement
or some philosophical point I was making, somebody would
stop me and say, "I really love the way your voice sounds. I
really love the way you're using your voice."

Oh, get out. If they only knew, I love their voices, too!
But of course we've been hearing American voices—I can't
remember when I *didn't* hear American voices in my life.
Many Americans have just started to recognize I'm
Australian. When I first went to the United States, people
would often say to me, "Are you English?" When the
answer was "No," they'd say, "Oh, Boston?"

Now many Americans say, "Oh, you're Australian."
I've stopped saying, "How did you know?" because the
answer was always *Crocodile Dundee*.

Australians are very rude to Americans sometimes, I'm
sorry to say. I think that's part of the territory of being a
more powerful culture. You kind of catch the flak for being
perceived as one of the most powerful cultures in the world.
So you end up getting all the criticism.

American students tell me Australians comment that
Americans have big teeth. Hollywood and television stars
like Farrah Fawcett and Robert Redford and Tom Selleck
have pretty impressive teeth. That is a common Australian
perception. Probably Americans have impressive teeth
because you've got wonderful dental care. Of course, dental
care has to do with the wealth of a society.

It is partly also that Australian aesthetic standards have
always defined themselves against perfection. That is to say,
Australians have always regarded a little bit of roughness, a
lack of smoothness and polish as being real and very honest.
We become suspicious of something too perfect.

It's a really weird sort of perception that Americans are
faster and brasher and sexier. American students will
comment about Australian films, "Oh, it's an Australian
movie. When do they get their clothes off?" If Americans
say to Australians, "There's a lot of sex in your movies,"

Australians will instantly say, "Oh, that's American influence."

That's really interesting because my perception of Americans—although I guess America has one of the pornography capitals of the world these days—is that they're far more modest and prudish and conventional in most matters than Australians are. Australians never think that is the case. So it is kind of strange to regard themselves in some senses as much more old-fashioned than Americans.

The other objection Australians will tell you constantly is that Australia is very Americanized. Now this is fascinating, because I've yet to meet an American person who thinks Australia is like America. But Australians expect you will think that. That's probably because of McDonald's and KFC.

In my view, all those signs of Americanization do not equal America. There's a perception in Australian culture that if we go on like this for another 100 years, Australia will turn into the United States. But if we give it another 200 million people in 100 years, it still will *never* happen.

There's a very interesting negativity in Australia, too. There's an assumption that things will probably turn out badly. There are also interesting reasons for this. And you can think about those and ask about them while you're here.

As we're so very fond of pointing out, one of the favorite responses of Australians, when you ask them how they are, is to say, "Not too bad." Whichever way you examine it, it means that their perception is that it *would* be bad, but today they're not too bad. The traditional American response to the greeting is to say, "I'm fine" or "I'm great."

Think of all the American slang Australians are trying on these days, like "awesome." That didn't last very long. You know, when I take American students to see a movie or a play, we come out and I say, "How was it?" They say, "Awesome!" I feel embarrassed. Whereas, an Australian would say, "It wasn't too bad." That's an appropriate response, to me.

I think the Australians of the 1980s and '90s are trying on a different set of values. By the way, one of the interesting things that's happening right now is the huge

growth of recovery books and self-help books in Australia.
You know, the books that tell you 50 ways to organize your
day, your marriage, your bad back and so on. Australians
are buying those books in great numbers now.

Up until this period, Australians would have regarded
those with great suspicion as being typical of all the worst
things in American culture. I think in this economic
recession, people are saying, "OK, our way hasn't worked
up until now, let's try something new."

One of the things Australians also will assume about you
is that you're all city dwellers. Some people come to
Australia and they say, "Gosh, Sydney is the biggest city
I've ever seen." Australians will say, "Oh, yeah. Right."

Of course, if you're from the hills in Kentucky, it may
be the biggest city you've seen. But Australians will think
that you're lying, because they're sure you all live in New
York or Los Angeles or Miami or Chicago or Dallas or
Beverly Hills. Why do we think that? Television. Apart from
Little House on the Prairie, we see all of you living in cities.

Now look at *Crocodile Dundee* where you've got this
ridiculous image where Australia equals the country and
Walkabout Creek and America equals Manhattan. It's kind
of two separate sets of values.

When Mick Dundee flies from Australia to New York,
notice he doesn't pass through Sydney or Melbourne, or any
of the boring airports you pass through to get to New York.
He flies straight from the desert of Walkabout Creek. I don't
know of any place in Australia where you can do that! That's
film's fancy geography.

Australians will assume you all eat junk food and only
junk food. Australians will assume all your television is
junk, whereas you know the truth (about cable and the wide
variety of documentaries and informational programming, in
addition to the entertainment).

They assume you've probably all been mugged. John
Lyons is a highly respected journalist, and he published an
article in the *Sydney Morning Herald* last year that was
typical of this attitude. What he reported, and I'm sorry this
is quite a grotesque example, was a scene in the United
States where a man raped his three-year-old daughter on the
hood of a car in the traffic in Manhattan. And the passersby

looked on. Stood there and watched. I do not believe it. I
simply do not believe this happened. But it's an amazing,
sensational, horrifying story.

Australians will assume that you're all great talkers, and
as I said earlier, your teeth are something to be suspicious
of. Assumptions.

You'll find some main themes in Australian children's
books. Traditionally, there is the kind of meeting of the
people and the land. This goes way back as a kind of
confrontation, a kind of a battle. Traditionally, from a
European point of view, it was the kind of venture that was
unexplainable or maybe even hostile. Not well understood.
Unfriendly, in a way.

A very strong feeling in Australian children's literature,
from the early days right until the present, is adventure in the
bush. As I said to you earlier, this is partially explainable
because there is simply more land per person. For the
population, there's a lot of nature here.

In 1899, one of the classics of Australian children's
literature was *Dot and the Kangaroo*. It is really a sort of
Alice in Wonderland set in the Australian bush. Dot is a little
girl who gets lost in the bush and meets a kangaroo. The
kangaroo gives her some berries to eat and puts her in its
pouch and takes Dot around the Australian countryside,
pointing out to her all these strange new sights. It explains
the trees, explains the berries, explains the flowers, explains
the Aborigines.

The kangaroo says that a lot of people talk about who the
real Australians are. Well, the kangaroo explains to Dot, the
real Australians are the plants and the animals of this
continent. Not even the Aborigines are real Australians, the
kangaroo says, because they kill kangaroos. The only
difference between Aboriginal people and white people is
that at least Aboriginal people kill kangaroos only for food.

From early on, there's a strong sense of the power of the
land and the need for environmental conservation. It occurs
in children's literature much earlier than in adult literature.
Jeannie Baker is one of the Australians who is still very
much in that tradition of understanding the special qualities
of the Australian environment and the need to preserve it.

Very, very often it's one of the oldest themes in Australian
children's literature.

On top of that, there are the family stories. This happens
in the United States, too, in the sense that there was often a
family with some strange things happening outside in the
night. They had to gather around the Victorian hearth, that
would be a kind of warm and friendly place. And there
would be a hostile world out there.

A typical story has this Victorian mother sitting with her
children gathered around her knee telling spooky stories
about Aborigines in order to drive home the importance of
the family unit and the house as a protection.

There is a continuing fascination with the Aboriginal
people from the earliest children's literature in the 19th
century. Aboriginal people were portrayed either as
bogeymen, people to be frightened of, or as comic
characters. "Bogeyman" is actually a word derived from an
Aboriginal term, bogy or devil man, in the first place.

The first Australian children's book, *A Mother's
Offering,* published in 1841, portrayed the Aboriginal people
as terrifying people who would kill you or poison you or
stick spears in your ears and so on if you went outside your
front door.

The theme that Aboriginal people were frightening, were
some kind of devils out to kill you, alternates with the
treatment of Aboriginal people as comic, kind of a joke. The
Billabong books early this century typify this view. Then
adult literature portrays them basically as alcoholics.

Frankly, the stereotypical treatment in Australia of
Aboriginal people is shameful. We've shown a total lack of
understanding of Aboriginal people until quite recently.

It's really important that you not look at the color of
Aboriginal people's skins and associate them with African-
Americans. They're much more comparable with Native
Americans. I think American society has very interesting
parallels.

Before European people moved to Australia, there was a
view, of course, that everything would be reversed. If you
had people on the other side of the world, where the seasons
were reversed, then maybe all kinds of behavior were
reversed, too. There were humorous theories that people

here walked upside-down. That they all lived in upside-down houses. As one commentator put it, "children ruled their parents and wives lay uppermost."

You won't find very much about sexual behavior in Australian literature for children or adults, interestingly. But you will find quite a lot about children being rebellious and different.

At the end of the 19th century, some of the classics like *Seven Little Australians* start off with a warning. They say something like, "if you're reading this book to read about model children, and ordinary children, forget it because there's no such thing in Australia." And *Seven Little Australians* goes on to say nature is different in Australia. It's rebellious. The bushes and trees are different from the usual, so naturally the people's behavior is different.

This is a very useful theme, of course, because any children's writer knows the first thing you have to do, if you want to get any interest at all, is get rid of their parents. Get rid of them either by killing them off or giving them something to do in the shopping mall or whatever else. Then you can have some real action with the kids. This theme of the rebelliousness and differentness of children goes from the beginning right through to now. I know there are naughty American children in American literature, but children who are a bit naughty are the norm in Australian literature. Very few Pollyannas or Rebeccas here!

We were talking a little earlier in the coffee room about differences in Australian and New Zealand culture. One of the differences is the strong Irishness of Australian culture and the anti-Anglo aspect that brings. Of course, tied into that is the rebelliousness. The desire to kind of stick your tongue out. You'll find this a lot in Australian satire and Australian writing for children.

From the 1970s on in children's literature, there's a very strong concern with the outsider, the person who's different from all the others. This is a fascinating thing to have emerged in Australian literature because of the very strong traditional concern in Australian culture with conformity and with the group. This also meant a certain lack of choice.

Australians read the American comic strips and cartoons where there were fabulous diners. They always seemed to make layer cakes a foot high and there always seemed to be an apple pie sitting on the windowsill.

When I first went to an American diner—this was quite a few years ago—you could get for 99 cents: two eggs and a muffin and coffee and bacon. I was just staggered by the price. It was so cheap, I couldn't believe it.

Then the waitress came up to me and she said, "How would you like your eggs?"

I thought, "You mean there's an option? I get a *choice?* For 99 cents?"

I said, "What are the choices?" And she started with about six versions of what you could do with your eggs. I just couldn't believe it. I knew back home in Australia there was one way they came off the grill. And if you didn't like it, tough luck. That's how everyone had eggs in this country. There was no choice about it.

You'll find as you go round hotels and restaurants here, a lot of that has changed. In most of the restaurants, you'll get your choices. But it's not a traditional Australian thing.

So it is very interesting in this period with the concern of the outside person. It is also the period in Australian culture where Australians are most concerned with the idea of being a multicultural society.

There was a celebration from the mid-1970s onward of the kind of experiment the Canadians were so proud of at one stage. And that is of being what you call the melting pot. One of the continuing themes you'll hear on television while you're here is, "Isn't it wonderful that none of the troubles in Sarajevo have been imported into Australia by Yugoslav-Australians?" That's a really important and continuing theme, and is played out in interesting ways particularly by writers for older readers and young adults in recent years.

Basically, Australian children's literature is dominated by a realist style of writing. With the whole history of Australian writing for children, you'd have to say the writing is realist in its style, in its use of language. That is, it places a great deal of emphasis on the plainness of the language, the plainness of the storytelling, the attitude that "I'm telling you what really happens out there."

Why the basic realism? Who knows. There are so many reasons. The importance of science in the development of European culture in Australia was one influence. It was all those botanists and astronomers and people who were sent here to write down and draw and report back on this strange country.

Sometimes when I'm outside Australia and see films about Australia, I think I'm living in a zoo. How can the Australian continent have more species of birds than any other continent on earth? Yet we live with them all the time. We take for granted the fact that we live in a hothouse of exotic species—strange plants and animals that the rest of the world is fascinated with.

It's so strange to go to a market in New York and see a parrot selling for $2,000. Those are the same parrots that farmers here are killing with sticks because they're driving them crazy eating the wheat and corn.

That aspect of being surrounded by exotic species led to the feeling we didn't really need to make up stories. There was a whole lot made up by nature for us here. You just had to write it down.

Australia has an outdoors climate. What is valued traditionally in European-Australian culture are the things of the body—physical pursuits like swimming, biking, horse riding, whatever it is. Work was valued above sitting at home reading by lamp light and making up stories and writing them.

We are not, in some writers' views, people of imagination and poetry and writing and so forth. Maybe the strength of Australian culture in those areas is in adversity. I don't know. A few of the Australian playwrights say Australians are traditionally suspicious of poetry and the imagination.

Even so, Australians write and Australians read. You know, there's only one English speaking population better at buying books than Australia and that's New Zealand. Quite staggering. And Australians don't realize that. They're still so locked into their sport and all sorts of physical activities.

The Australia Council is having a big campaign to tell us by statistics and so forth that Australians go to more arts-

related activities than sporting-type activities and have done
so for a long time. But Australians don't believe it. They
simply don't believe it.

The major change in Australian children's literature in the
1980s and 1990s has been a movement towards fantasy and
towards works of the imagination. We're focusing on the
way language can create reality and invent experience. Why
is that? Maybe film, television, video and music video have
had a lot of influence on kids and the way kids see things.
All of those things have developed a very sophisticated
literary visual literacy.

If you look at music video, for example, it throws in so
many visual images in such bizarre ways that you can't
possibly think that this is realism or factual reportage. If it is,
I don't know what it is reporting.

Also I think Aboriginal perspectives have been important
in the trend toward imaginative storytelling. Starting in the
1970s and as the bicentenary drew on in 1988, Aboriginal
voices became stronger and stronger in the society.
Basically, the bicentenary operated as a kind of goad, a
threat to Aboriginal culture in Australia. The bicentenary
slogan was "Celebrate in '88." Many Aboriginal people said,
"What is there to celebrate? Your people came here 200 years
ago and robbed us of our sovereignty."

During that period, Aboriginal voices actually got
stronger and brought to us that whole realm of imagination,
their stories of dreaming. Their traditional stories were not
just about the everyday, the day to day. They're about what
we would see, if it's not an offensive term, as the fantastic.
The metaphysical. And that's been a very important thing.

The bicentenary had another interesting effect on non-
Aboriginal Australians and that was to give renewed force to
nationalism in publishing for children. At the same time
Aboriginal culture was giving a great strength to the
metaphysical, non-Aboriginal culture was developing the
jokey side of it, the very nationalistic imagery and so forth.

In one way, the person who was most responsible for
that was Mem Fox, the author, along with Julie Vivas, the
illustrator, with *Possum Magic*. They featured a sort of
cheekiness, a kind of a satiric attention. And very
nationalistic—a lot of Australianness in the work. Very, very

strongly child-centered. The kids love this sort of cheeky imagery.

The style they set up for the Australian picture book, via the publishing house Omnibus, in the 1980s, really developed a very strong identity and particular characteristics.

Typically, the books were the square shape and that was new. They used a lot of white space. That's quite interesting if you want to intellectualize it. I think it may be seen as a reflection on the psychic space in Australia. This was a very uncommon kind of page with very strong and fluid images on it, very typical of the Omnibus style.

Another writer who changed our ways of seeing was Patricia Wrightson. She's been writing since the 1950s, and she's still Australia's only children's writer to have been awarded the Hans Christian Andersen medal. Patricia Wrightson really replaced Ivan Southall, frankly, as the most important, the most prestigious Australian writer for young people in the 1970s.

Ivan Southall wrote in the tradition of the adventure story, which goes way back in the 19th century and earlier. Children up against strange odds: the flood, the fire, the air disaster, the disaster with drums of poison in the night. All these situations have psychological dimensions and symbolic meanings. So basically, once again, the stories were about people against the natural world and against disaster.

Patricia Wrightson, though, put her characters under spiritual odds in the mode of the Aboriginal people. At first she used non-Aboriginal characters. Later in her works she was able to use the interesting situation of an Aboriginal person coming up against their own heritage. By means of a stone ax or some legend they heard or by some other link, her characters would meet the whole world of Aboriginal metaphysics, the whole Dreaming. And it would be terrifying sometimes.

Everybody's been wanting to know for 30 years what Aboriginal people think about Patricia Wrightson. She has often said, "In a way it doesn't matter. I'm not writing for Aboriginal people. They know their own stuff and if they want to write their own stuff, that's up to them; I'm not writing for them; I'm writing for non-Aboriginal people. The whole meaning of Australian culture is there if only they'd realize it and tap into it."

Others like Diana Kidd or Jeannie Adams are non-Aboriginal writers and artists writing about Aboriginal subjects. This is a very hot issue at the moment. Many people think it's quite inappropriate, and they should stop doing it. I think I'm probably one of them.

Jeannie Adams' answer is that she's doing it because the Aboriginal people can't really do it themselves. Diana Kidd's answer is that she's had approval from the Aboriginal people. So that's one of the issues you'll find as you go around now.

Patricia Wrightson opened the way for writers like Lilith Norman to write fantasies. Her book *A Dream of Seas* is one of the most beautiful books Australians ever produced. And her new book, *The Paddock,* her first picture book, is also in that kind of writing. It doesn't deal directly with Aboriginal subject matter. Instead, it opens up the whole metaphysical world in the way that Patricia Wrightson had. Patricia Wrightson also enabled Victor Kelleher, one of the other leading fantasy writers of our day, to write. Victor Kelleher's book *Del-del*, which was shortlisted for the Book of the Year for Older Readers in 1992, is a kind of thriller. It starts off in urban Sydney with a child who is speaking backwards and he's hiding in a closet and doing all sorts of strange and disturbing things.

I couldn't put this book down. It just grabbed me from the first. This is like a movie—quite frightening. And this is quite unusual for Victor Kelleher in some ways, although the middle of the book goes back into legend.

Typically, he goes back into the past using the European past or medieval legend or myth. Or he projects into the future in a book like *Taronga,* where it's a sort of post-nuclear holocaust world and the only safe place would be the zoo. The whole world outside the zoo is the animal world and everything's reversed.

Patricia Wrightson said she never writes about good and evil. She says she writes about being out of place. She's interested in preserving the natural environment as it is and humans in that place. So she's a kind of ecologist.

Victor Kelleher does write about good and evil. The interesting thing is that he always deliberately confuses what is good and what is evil. What you thought is good turns out to be a bit evil and what you thought to be evil turns out to be a bit good. This is fascinating and important to me in a period when advertisers have persuaded teenagers, particularly, that the image is the reality. If you wear the right shoes, if you wear the right top, if you wear the right sunglasses, you can say you are that person.

Victor Kelleher's confusing of stereotypes is so important for kids. I think that his books will help them to question whether wearing Oakley Blades is going to make them the particular kind of person that the advertisers say it will.

Science fiction has never been very popular or important in children's writing in Australia. In 1986, Gillian Rubenstein made a big impression with her book *Space Demons*. It was one of those books that was a sleeper. It was published in October. But it wasn't until four or five months later that anybody started to realize it was quite some book.

Space Demons is about some kids playing with a video game and they get sucked into the game. There's this frightening moment when Andrew suddenly has a gun in his hand, and he has to go into the video game in order to pull his friends out.

It was interesting because people said, well, here's technology. Here's modern Hollywood lasers and all that sort of stuff in literature for kids. It was fascinating at first because of the subject matter she appeared to be writing about.

But it became immediately apparent that high technology wasn't Gillian Rubenstein's main interest. She is more interested in the emotions, in learning to control the emotions, in the independence of her girl characters and so on.

She's gone on to become one of the most important fantasy writers in Australia. *Beyond the Labyrinth* is a book which has caused more trouble than it's worth in some ways. It's a fantastic book. But two or three paragraphs in the book have the "F" word in them. This was deliberately used in quite a sophisticated way.

It was used by an adult to a child. The adult had suffered the death of a child. When she sees another child playing in the area where her own child died, she screams this abuse at her. Interestingly, at one point later in the book, the children start using the language themselves and there's a little message in it about those words.

Well, for various reasons, some people have taken this as a license to publish four letter words in Australian children's books. And that's one of the issues in publishing for children. I think it's a dead issue, but it's been here for a little while.

What happened to the real-life adventure story for children in Australia? I think it turned into Allan Baillie's stories, which have a very psychological kind of bent. They're almost like Ivan Southall for the '90s.

Feminism adopted the realist stories and gave us Robin Klein, who became the 1980s leading star of Australia's children's writer's. Robin Klein wrote about very adventurous girls, witty girls, girls doing things that are unexpected, girls telling us all about life from their point of view. And it's usually very, very funny and very cranky.

She usually has a girl telling you from inside her own head what life is like. This girl is always clever. She's always very adult in her humor, and she usually despises the people around her. It's interesting to hear children's own voices being heard.

Paul Jennings is like Robin Klein with his humor, with his access to the reluctant reader, with the simplicity of his language. He also turned on its head the publisher's dictum, the publisher's wisdom, that short stories don't sell.

Like Robin Klein, he deals in funny surfaces, but there's a lot of subtlety underneath and a lot of people have missed that. Like Robin Klein, he missed out on all the awards, even though he's the children's favorite. He never gets the book of the year award. Robin Klein finally got the award when she became serious in *Came Back to Show You I Could Fly.* This is a really interesting feature of the 1980s.

Books by Morris Gleitzman, a journalist and columnist,
are funny and popular. He writes not in a literary style, but
in a style that will make kids laugh and appeals to me.

Bob Graham's wonderful picture books, like *Greetings
from Sandy Beach,* are typical of this, too. My favorite *The
Wild* is actually a beautiful book. It is my idea of a writer's
book. It's a really lovely portrait of ordinary family life that
shows adults and children. Very, very warm. It explores the
meaning of the inside and the outside, which is a very old
Australian children's literature theme.

Bob Graham uses comic strip cartoon-style caricatures
that are very accessible to people who don't like to read
much. They're great fun. They've got domestic detail.
They're very beautifully written. Again, it's extremely
popular and until quite recently, not awarded any awards.

That's a really neat feature of writing children's books
for children in the 1980s. The popularity of the writer. The
accessibility of the writer to kids. The child-centeredness of
it and yet an increasing polarization from adult values and so
on. There is a splitting off of children's literature popular
with children and children's literature approved by librarians
and judges and people like that.

Literary art books are basically supported by the
educational market and specialist book sellers and the
Children's Book Council. High-quality, worthy, serious
stuff. An art object beautiful to hold and so on. These books
are often something adults wished they'd had when they
were young. They are a reaction against television and
popular culture by parents and adults.

They also are a reaction by adults who are fleeing from
adult books. Increasingly, adults are reading children's
books and that is producing children's books adults will
read. This has influenced recent publishing in this country.

When I look at your most popular illustrators, Chris Van
Allsburg, for example, or William Joyce, I think of adult
appeal. The 1930s style those illustrators are using means
nothing to kids. It means nostalgia to you. The time when
values were real and people weren't being mugged. It's a
whole different world.

There's some of that in Australian children's publishing. You see a book out there called *The Very Best of Friends,* which has the soft style and those warm values—home, family, animals and so forth. The soft style versus the popular and the romance and the thriller. Actually in Australia, we have more of the mystery than the thriller. I think that's interesting.

When you have a look at the shortlist for book of the year, you will see the qualities I'm talking about. You'll see the importance of the letter form in children's writing with the whole novel written as a letter or a diary. All these things that kind of split children's literature into two. You'll see books like *The Wolf* which adults like, and books like *Letters from the Inside* which adults are very worried about. I'm very worried about it, because I don't think it's a children's *book*. Children reviewing it around the country are saying this book is about my real life, and you look at their smiling faces and think, "No it's not."

Which brings us back to stereotypes, the way we see things I guess—and that's where all this talk of Australians, Americans, children and books started!

JEANNIE BAKER

Jeannie Baker is an illustrator and author of picture books. Her collage illustrations are rich in detail and texture, and her books with few or no words are also deep and rich in meaning. We were there when she won the Australian Children's Book Council Book of the Year Award for *Window,* a wordless picture book, which she describes as being about change. She illustrated her talk with slides of her collages and scenes that inspired her illustrations when she met our group at the Rozelle Writers' Centre in Sydney.

I'm going to tell you a bit about how my work developed and then talk in more detail about some of my books. I'll start by talking a bit about drawing as I see that as the basis of all my work.

I grew up in England and went through art school there. Part of our course in art school was life drawing. The first art school I went to used models I found interesting—like boxers, pregnant women, and old people.

I went on to specialize in graphic design and in our life drawing classes, as part of this course, we had mostly attractive young women posing in very strange positions on chairs and tables. I could never really quite get into it because it seemed so unnatural. So I started not going to my life drawing classes.

Instead, I wandered the streets and looked for people I found interesting. When I'd find them I'd ask them, "Can I do a drawing of you?" In this way, I got, I suppose, quite relaxed and confident about drawing in public and about walking up to strangers and asking if I could draw them. It was very unusual for someone to refuse to let me do a drawing, probably because they were flattered that I wanted to.

One of the places where I used to do my drawings was a particular transport cafe where a lot of unemployed people would hang out. At first they were really suspicious of me

97

because they thought I was a police informer. Then they got used to me.

I found that—and it's still true now—I can only do work that's successful for me—if I'm really interested in what I'm doing. This was a lesson I learned at about that time.

At the same time at college I was doing a lot of painting. My paintings were miniatures, and they were very textured and abstract—I built up the paint a lot. I would get part of the way through one of those paintings and I would start feeling uncomfortable with it because I could see it could be vastly improved in the way it was arranged. So I started cutting out parts of the painting and rearranging them. The very nature of my doing that changed them from being pure painting into being collages. That's how my collages started.

I would spend hours building up textures with paint. Often I would use the paint in a way it shouldn't really be used, and the paint would crack, and I'd have all sorts of problems.

I thought rather than paint texture, why not use real texture! This is the first collage I made using real, found textures. I called it *Autobiography of a Walk Along the Seashore*. Everything on it was collected from the beach. I used things like different colored sands from different parts of the beach. There's pieces of tin that had got rusty and eroded and looked interesting to me. Pieces of wood that had been washed up. Different kinds of shells and seaweed used together in an abstract way.

During my final year at college, I thought maybe I could use real textures in a representational way. This was when I did my first book, which was later published as *Grandfather*.

I never ever thought it would be published. It was something I did purely because that's what I wanted to do. I wrote, designed and illustrated the book. In this illustration, I used things like pieces of old plaster peeled from real walls, as I love the textures and natural effects—the cracks, the erosion, within the plaster.

The door and the window frame in the illustration are made up of old paint peeled from peeling doors and window frames. So, again, you get the texture I find exciting, including places where you see paint from where it was painted before, where the top layer has peeled off.

I feel the graphic design course was a wonderful background for the kind of work I do now, and it gave me some confidence to be involved in the design of my books.

When I left art school, people were interested in my collage work because it was different. So I started getting collage commissions to do illustrations for magazines. I also got various commissions from advertising agencies.

When my work started being reproduced in magazines, sometimes people would contact the art director because they were interested in buying the original. So I suddenly found myself in a slightly different position. People were actually interested in buying my originals.

In this way I was introduced to a lady who became a sort of patron of mine. She had a big mansion in the English countryside. She'd show me a room in this mansion and say, "Look, I'd like you to do a collage for here and you can do whatever you like." I even did collages for her bathrooms.

So for someone who had just left art school being given that sort of freedom was a fantastic opportunity. At this stage, too, I was offered an exhibition by a London gallery. For about six months I did nothing other than pieces I really wanted to do for this exhibition.

At this stage I was in a strange position. I was working purely in collage. But I was working in a number of different "worlds." And I was thinking slightly differently, depending on the "world" I was working for. I had total freedom if I was doing a piece for exhibition. I would be very confined if I were doing a piece for an ad agency. I was confined by the text when I was doing a piece to illustrate a magazine article. I was also writing and illustrating children's picture books.

I started thinking about this and wondering if there was a way that I could do work that was more personally satisfying to me, something that worked in a number of these "worlds." By this time I'd moved to live in Australia. It was 1977 and I got a grant to work on a special project. So for awhile I didn't have to think so carefully about money. The grant gave me the luxury of space and time to develop my work.

I developed a project that centered around Hyde Park which is a park in central Sydney. In the park I particularly recognized individuals who were characters some people might call eccentric. For many of them, their home is the park.

To give a focus to the book part of the project that developed, I used a real old lady who goes to the park every day to feed the pigeons. Gradually, I developed a book with no words. I said everything I wanted to say clearly with the pictures.

But the feedback I got from my publishers (at that stage they were in England) was that you really need to write words, because books without words don't sell very well. So I was put in a situation where words were an after thought, which for me isn't the way I usually go about doing a book. I usually work out my words and images together and I try to say different things with each.

I felt very frustrated. First of all, I wrote a lot of very obvious words which were already in the pictures, but it wasn't working for me. And then I thought, "Ok, I'll take this as a challenge. How can I use words and say something I'm not saying in the images?"

Then I had the idea of the words being the pigeon lady's private world—her thoughts. So I thought of the words as abstract illustrations to the visual text.

Once I'd set the scene, I interspersed images on white space with no background, with other images of the park, which are very detailed and dense. I thought this balance of contrast important.

I designed this book from the beginning so that a number of the images were double or single page spreads that could fit together to make a larger image. This became the main image—the focal image—in the exhibition which I later had of the work. This complex image was also reproduced as a print. In this way with this project I was working in several different "worlds," which is what I'd hoped to do.

After spending two-and-a-half years working on these Hyde Park images, I really felt I needed a total change of environment. I had a chance to go to New York. The Visual

Arts Board of the Australia Council has a studio and living space in Soho and it was offered to me. After being there a few weeks, I started thinking about what I could make of this experience. First of all I thought I would like to make a project out of the subway.

I always start my projects by trying to get as in touch with my feelings and with the particular environment as I can. So apart from reading up about the subway and finding out about its history, I explored just about every subway line there is in New York. I'd spend all my daytime hours on the subway, riding the trains—thinking.

At the end of two weeks of riding the subway, I felt totally depressed. And I thought, with the amount of time it takes me to do a project, I would drown in the negative images if I focused on something like the subway. I started looking for something that was more uplifting to me.

I lived in New York for a year. Apart from feeling very lucky to have had that experience, I found it a very tough year. I found New York at street level a very tough place and, in many ways, it was hard for me to come to terms with.

But I found a very different world on the rooftops of New York. Often there were roof-gardens on the rooftops as people didn't have space for gardens down at street level. Children would play on the rooftops, and they would put their nicknames on their chimney pots so their friends from streets away could see where they lived.

I found the rooftops had a lot of character, and I found the tops of the New York skyscrapers beautiful and ethereal, like fairy tale castles.

So I gradually developed the book *Home in the Sky,* which is very focused around New York City rooftops. I used homing pigeons as a vehicle to take the viewer through different parts of New York I found exciting.

I think of the image of the pigeons in their coops as a bit like New Yorkers in their apartments. Mike, the character in my story who keeps homing pigeons, is actually based on a man I met in New York.

I returned to Australia in 1984—and I came back looking to do a project set in the wilderness—probably as a reaction to spending nearly a year in New York. I had a very strong feeling for doing a project set in a rain forest.

Of all the environments on earth, the tropical rain forest is the most complex, meaning that you get the greatest number of different kinds of plants and animals living together in one community. There's not much rain forest left in the world.

At the back of my mind was the mention of a tropical rain forest called Daintree in Queensland. What is even more special about this particular forest is the way the rain forest comes right down to the beach like a great green wall. Just off the beach is the Great Barrier Reef and a whole new environment of a coral reef.

Since I was thinking of doing a project in the rain forest, it was important that I go up there and explore it for myself. I gave a workshop in Cairns, which meant I got a free trip. Cairns, the nearest town to the Daintree, is about three hours drive south of the rain forest.

A number of the people I worked with in Cairns were quick to point out to me that the rain forest was, in fact, very dangerous. They told me that there were wild pigs and snakes that might attack and drug growers who might shoot on sight, among other dangers. And that I really shouldn't go. But if I had to, to go with company and take a gun.

Well, you can imagine after hearing stories like that, I wasn't sure I wanted to go anymore! Then I thought, I'll go and talk to people actually living in the forest. If they tell me the same things, I won't stay.

I had a contact who had property at the Daintree, and he gave me permission to put up my tent on his land. So this became my base camp. After being there and talking to people who actually did live there, I felt a lot more comfortable. They laughed at most of the stories I'd been told and put things into clearer perspective.

It's like being in New York City. You don't walk in certain places. Gradually, I became more and more confident and I started going for long walks into the forest on my own. I had really good maps with me and a compass. I had never used a compass before, but I had the instructions with me.

Initially, I planned to take a tent in my rucksack, but it turned out to be quite heavy. Just carrying food enough for several days along with a sketchbook and camera was heavy enough. I found I was okay just to take a sheet of plastic to wrap myself up in at night.

It was hot, but I wasn't there in the rainy season, so it was comfortable. It was important to do a lot of exploring, as everywhere I went was different as is the nature of the tropical rain forest.

I tried to make a point of the differences in the book that developed (*Where the Forest Meets the Sea*). Every tree I showed in the images is different to the tree next to it.

I also spent time with Aboriginals who live in a reserve north of the Daintree forest. They were descendants of the Aborigines whose home was the forest—who lived totally in the forest. I had permission to go in there and talk to some of those people.

A family of these Aborigines spent a day with me walking in the forest and talking a bit about the forest from their perspectives. They pointed out plants that would have been eaten there.

Quite soon after being there, I decided I wanted to make something of this experience and started thinking about ideas for a project. When I start a project, ideas come very slowly. It usually starts with a feeling and I've learned to rely on my intuition as much as anything.

As I said earlier, both words and images grow together. Usually I start in a small way. I start with just one small sheet of paper, and I write down a few key words and feelings and scribble some images. Then I start drawing little boxes which I think of as pages of the book. Gradually, I develop ideas until I become more clear about what it is I want to say.

As my ideas became clearer, the boxes depicting pages gradually grow larger until they finally become the size in which I will finally work. I work out all my ideas initially in those drawings. This also is the way I communicate with my publisher.

So I work on these drawings, thinking of the book very much as a whole, before focusing too much on detail. I go over and over and over it. I did about five layout versions of the book before I felt it was working well enough for me to want to send it to Susan Hirschman, my editor at Greenwillow.

The initial reaction from Susan was, "You need to take it further." So then I had to work some more on it and think about it from different angles. It obviously wasn't working well enough. It was only on the third layout I did for Susan that it began to work.

At this point too, I was thinking of the book, but I was also thinking of the overall project. I was hoping it would work in other ways too.

I had an idea of it working as an animated film. I liked the idea of actually animating into the collages. I didn't know if I could get it off the ground, but at this initial stage I wanted to leave this option open. So I designed the double-page spread illustrations in the book to the same proportion as the cinema wide screen.

Later, Film Australia decided they would like to produce the animation and as I had very strong ideas about the ways I wanted it to work, they let me direct the film. It was only 10 minutes long, but it was a really good experience.

Also in my mind was the idea of some of the images working in an exhibition. So even at the earliest stages of the project, I was developing some of these images with the book and the film and exhibition also in mind.

I got to the point where I worked out what I wanted to say in the book and in the project as a whole. But in doing that I realized I didn't have enough information about some of the details. So I made a second trip back to the rain forest to get the details right, to look at some things more closely and to collect some specimens.

In the rain forest, everything is giant, on a huge scale, and my work is miniature, so it didn't work for me to use many of the actual materials I could find there. Mostly, I had to look for things that were much smaller in scale, more to the proportion with which I was working. I made a point of depicting particular plants like fan palms which are everywhere in the forest. If I tried to depict the rain forest without putting in things like the fan palms, it wouldn't have been the Daintree. So I collected a few real things like that even though they were out of scale so I could depict shapes and details correctly.

Of all the rain forests on earth, the Daintree is one of the least changed. Quite recently, the most primitive flowering plant yet found on earth was found in one small part of one valley in the Daintree. We're still discovering new species in our rain forests.

I wanted the book to try to get across the incredible age of this forest. That's why I've called the boat *Time Machine,* because one could liken the trip to the rain forest to stepping back in time more than a million years to the time when dinosaurs would have been there.

One of the other ways in which I explored the rain forest was by living with a family who lived in the forest far from anyone else. There were three young boys in this family who had been born and grown up in the rain forest.

Mostly, the children didn't wear clothes because it's so hot and there's no one else living near by. It was most comfortable not to wear clothes. Initially in the book I wanted the boy in my story to be naked. Not only was it realistic, but also I kept thinking about all the stories I'd been told about how dangerous this place was and what a different reality I found.

In the book I wanted to get across the feeling that the boy didn't feel threatened by the forest. One can see clothes as a barrier between us and the world. I wanted to take away that barrier, but Greenwillow felt that children wouldn't understand this. So reluctantly, I put a pair of shorts on the boy in the book.

In the film of *Where the Forest Meets the Sea,* I had total freedom, so I took the opportunity to show the boy naked. I find it interesting to watch children watching the film. Little children, especially, often start giggling because the boy's got no clothes on. That's made me realize that my publisher was right. When they're giggling, their concentration is being broken and in this way they're missing more important elements of the story.

I designed the book so that a number of pages—a number of parts—could come together as a composite piece, which would be the focal image in the traveling exhibition of the work.

Anyone who goes to Daintree can't help but think about the changes that are taking place there.

The last time I was there was in 1985. Even then there were bulldozers and large pieces of land had been cleared for housing subdivisions. This was something I wanted to communicate in the book.

I leave the ending open as a question, because I'm hoping that people will decide for themselves what future they think this rain forest and other special places like it should have.

For a long time I'd wanted to do a book with no words. My latest picture book, *Window,* is a wordless picture book. This isn't a book I find easy to talk about. The first idea of *Window* is to convey to a young reader the nature of change and how small changes added to small changes can eventually result in a major change—the concept of exponential change.

This I thought would be a really good challenge for me. To do this, I gave the book a time frame against which changes can be measured, so I have the book covering the time period of one generation. In the first spread I show a mother looking out of a window with a baby in her arms. The final image shows that baby grown to be a father looking out of a window with his own baby in his arms.

The pages in between show the view from the first window at two-year intervals. When we go from page to page, the details change in particular patterns. First of all in the view we just see native bush. Then a dirt road gets pushed through and the garden becomes fenced. Then the first house appears. Then, you might notice, there are two houses, then four, then eight, then 16. With every two-year time frame, the number of buildings doubles, until it gets to the point where there isn't enough space to double the buildings any more. So the first skyscraper appears.

If we compare two adjacent pages, the change is small. But if we compare the first image to the final view from the same window, the change is major. These small incremental changes have added up to major change.

I see *Window* as a metaphor for our changing world. As the native forest is depleted bit by bit, similarly the native birds and animals are depleted, and if you look hard enough even insects are depleted.

Introduced animals such as cats increase. (Cats originated in other countries and were brought to Australia without their natural predators, which kept them from becoming pests in their native lands.) The cats next door keep having kittens until it gets to the point where there's something like 28 cats.

Initially, there are lots of birds. Then as the view is developed, the birds start diminishing. You might notice, if you look closely and if you know Australia, that the native birds are gone and the few birds that are left are introduced species. Finally, there aren't even any of these. In my mind, the boy misses the birds, so he hangs a knitted native bird from his window.

At the end of the book, where the grown boy reaches the point of completing the generation, he's depicted with his own child standing at the window of his new house looking out at the view, intended to be similar and parallel to the first window view, implying the beginning of a whole new cycle, only this time at a more advanced pace of change. You might notice that across the road already land has been cleared for a housing subdivision and you can see a silhouette of the city he's just left on the horizon.

Those changes depicted are essentially those happening in the neighborhood. But the view also incorporates the backyard of the house of the *Window* where you can see the boy as he grows up, being active and making changes there himself.

Here he's pulled down one of the native trees in his backyard with which to build himself a tree house. In this image he's trying to catch a bird with his slingshot.

I wanted to include this idea to convey how we each play a part in making small changes which contribute to the larger changes that we don't readily see at the time of our actions.

I can well expect that some or all of these concepts might not be properly grasped and understood by a child. But what I am confident in is that children do enjoy following details and patterns and they do constantly surprise me with their understanding of these concepts in *Window*. And where they have not been understood, I like the idea that as the children

grow older, they can return to the book and find more there
than they had previously seen.

I also like the way children can use a wordless book.
When a child tells an adult the story they see in the book, it
is often very different from the story that's in my mind as
I'm developing the book. I've had some, to me, really
strange stories that have evolved from the book as children
tell the story they see. That's one of the things about this
book that I'm happiest about.

ROBIN KLEIN

Robin Klein is a prolific and popular author who has written books for all age groups. She handles serious and light subjects with equal skill. Her wonderful sense of humor sparkled as naturally through her talk as it does through her books. She invited us to her large stone country house outside Belgrave near Melbourne in Victoria. A young family friend and aspiring author graciously served tea and sandwiches as we visited informally with the author after her presentation.

All the letters I get, including those little letters I get from America, start off with "Where do you get your ideas?" One thing you learn to do very early as a writer is to keep an idea book. There was a time before I went to sleep at night I'd write down in my idea book five interesting things I'd seen during the day. Ideas abound; they're everywhere. Everything's grist for your mill.

I think it is the way you train yourself when you know you're going to be a writer. How do you observe these things and take impressions? What were your childhood observations?

It's rather a lovely thing being a writer. I went with two other writers last week to Queenscliff down on the bay. We had five hours to kill, so we had this great walk and we were having a wonderful time. We burst into fits of laughter—on that walk there was something funny.

We went into an army fort where they trained anything above the rank of lieutenant colonel. Everything was so spotless. All the blades of grass were growing in the same direction—straight up as if they were standing at attention. We could just imagine there were all these privates out there every day mowing it and raking it and seeing that each blade was perfect.

They had two cannons at the fort. At one stage, about 1910, Australia thought Russia was going to invade. Very conceited really when you look back on it. So they've got two big cannons facing into the bay down there. I don't know how that would have held off the Russian navy.

These were the sort of things we saw. All these things were fascinating to us and could have been jotted down in an idea book and perhaps some time used in a story.

I have lots and lots of idea books. I jot down anything. I'll read just a few examples. "Seen from the train a tiny slice of green in a slum area no bigger than half a tennis court and a notice 'the Ethel Brown reserve'" and here I've got a note "Who was Ethel Brown." That developed into a little book called *Junk Castle*. I wrote that ages ago, and it might have slipped by if I hadn't jotted down what I saw.

Junk Castle came from just seeing from the train where those kids play. The idea developed into kids living in the inner city who build this castle out of junk. They make the nearby residents angry and end up defending their castle in military fashion. That has been a very successful book. It's been translated into four languages.

Another source of ideas is newspaper clippings. There was a case that occurred in 1980 in Melbourne. Two teenagers one day escaped from their home enclosed in a high fence and went to a neighbor. They were escaping from a man who belonged to a very strange religion indeed. He had trained his children to tertiary level in mathematics, but he thought the world was such a terrible place he wasn't going to have his children contaminated by it.

He had a family of 10 children living there. None of them had ever been to a supermarket. They didn't know what a movie house was. They had never gone to a school. The kids, of course, had to be educated all over again. I thought it was quite an interesting bit of news. So I saved that and months later I found another newspaper article much the same about a family in England.

Neighbors only suspected kids lived there because they heard music being played at night. Very late at night this man would bring all these white-faced children walking around the block for their exercise.

So I realized there are quite a lot of people living like that. From that I wrote a book called *People Might Hear You*. I think it's available in America.

It's about a girl whose guardian marries into a sect where the kid has to learn to adjust to it. I tried to write it first of all from the viewpoint of a child who knew nothing but that kind of life. But it was just too black and white with no nuances in it at all.

It was quite a strange book to write actually. When I was writing it I used to get this terrible sense of claustrophobia. I had to stop and go outside in the garden and then come back in to write.

I made a mistake with that. I left the ending open. I thought it was a very artistic kind of ending. I was very proud of it. I've got the girl and her friend on the bridge. They've managed to escape. The reader must decide whether they will be able to hold onto their freedom in the world outside.

Every child in Australia has written to scold me about this ending. They ask "Are you going to write a sequel?" and they send me alternative endings. I realized, watching television, they're used to having everything resolved in a clear cut way. So I feel quite embarrassed about that ending.

When you've got a store of ideas, you're ready to actually write a book. I start a master sheet of all the things— that's another idea—I must tell you about.

When my older daughter was 13, she suddenly went from being a tiny, little, skinny girl to looking like Helen of Troy. So I was Helen of Troy's mother.

She developed a beautiful figure. She had long golden hair. And she used to ride her brother's horse all around the neighborhood. So I had every young lad in the area coming and knocking on our door. And I started keeping a list of all her boyfriends.

One week's supply filled more than a page. And I started giving them marks from one to 10 on various characteristics. One rated minus three and I said, "Don't you bring that terrible boy into the house."

I saved those lists and when I was coming to write another book with a friend of mine called *The Lonely Hearts Club,* I used them to help create the main characters.

The Lonely Hearts Club was about two boys in a Catholic boarding school. Their one ambition in life is to meet young ladies. Because they're such excellent nerds, the girls won't have anything to do with them until they start a Lonely Hearts Club. So to get the characters of the two boys, all I had to do was go through the lists in that book.

When I come to write I always make a master sheet. When I have that master sheet, I type directly onto the word processor. I don't mind about form at all. All I want to do is get the structure. Like the scaffolding for a building. I've got to have that structure before I can work on it.

This master sheet is from a story about this girl who finds a genie in a bottle. In the kitchen and in between turning the chops and doing all the things I do as a householder, I write down all the names of things I could conceivably use in it—Arabic kinds of names, foods they would have eaten like pomegranates and dates and figs—everything I might use and if I don't use them I cross them out.

I've got that nucleus of the story about the kid who finds the bottle here on my master sheet. She rubs the bottle and the genie hops out. But he's rather a horrible genie. Of course, he's been locked up for so long he doesn't know the 20th century. Everything she asks him, he can't understand what she means.

She asks for a caravan, and she looks out into the backyard and there's a string of camels. That's what he understands by a caravan. She asks for a dishwasher for her mum, and there's a scream from mum in the kitchen. He's sent her a great big eight-foot tall slave with a scimitar.

Then she wants a video for her dad, and she tried to explain that her dad likes watching light entertainment. Suddenly, there's these three beautiful dancing girls sitting on dad's knee. One's rubbing his bald spot. Dad thinks this is a bit of all right. But mum is very annoyed because she thinks he met them all down at the football club and asked them home.

And the genie won't get rid of them. And this poor kid's got a houseful of weird things. That was just the basic idea of the story.

I'm actually a very messy writer. I have a friend who writes science fiction. He will sit at the word processor and write one perfect sentence and look at it for ten minutes and type the next, and it's all building blocks. By the end of 18 months, he has a book. He doesn't have to do any more work on it.

I do 25 drafts. Here I've got the first draft, and I'll just go through and correct it. I have to be quite ruthless—whole pages gone bad have to be cut. Then when it gets too messy to work on, I do another draft. I go through and refine it again and again.

It's really just like a process of woodworking. Sanding and polishing and sanding and polishing till you reach the stage where you can't really do too much more to it. At that stage I put it away for about three weeks or so and work on something else. Then I'll get it out.

It's like painting. When you paint a picture, you turn it to the wall for a few weeks. When you get it out after that period, all the faults will jump out at you. When I feel I really can't do much more to it, then I sort of top it off and send it in.

If it's accepted as a book, then I get back this horrible thing called an edited version from my publisher. In the edited version, my editor has written all these little changes that she wants.

By that time you're sick of the book. The editor is sick of the book. Everyone's sick of the book. But you've got to have the discipline to sit down, if necessary, and rewrite it in first person or put another chapter in.

Julie Watts is my editor. She's actually one of the best editors in Australia—she's marvelous. She lives just around the corner from me which is another bonus. I've learned to take a lot of notice of Julie. She has a very quiet way, and she asks so beautifully for the changes. She's got this lovely English chic voice, and she charms changes out of you.

If it's going to be an illustrated book, you've got an artist hard at work. They send you roughs of the things they're going to be doing in an illustrated book. It's really fascinating when you see the roughs. I haven't got a very good visual facility, I suppose you'd call it. I actually have to look at a thing and sometimes I think it looks terrible, but then I get the lovely color work and it looks fine. I've actually been very lucky with my artists.

The people at Penguin are very professional. They're very good actually about calling authors in to consult at every stage of the way. I've got clauses written into my contracts now that I've got to see at least the rough work. I'll see the rough work, and I'll see the color work. It does happen, though, that people can be bitterly disappointed in the artwork.

I've got one I really don't like. It's a rather uncomplicated little story about a little girl who finds an old bear. And I really don't like the artwork. It's just not the kind of artwork for a simple story. It's too bizarre. It might work quite well for older kids, but it's not working for five year olds. It's too—I really don't like it. I really was quite disappointed with it.

They sent me the rough pencil work, and I had reservations about it. That's when I should have stepped in and said, I didn't consider it appropriate. I thought perhaps the colors would brighten it up. But the color is a bit somber, too. I suppose that's just the luck of the draw. You're just very lucky to get a book published now.

When they've got it in color format, I get this sort of mocked up thing back. I think it's more for the color printers because it's got little guides that check their colors.

Most artists get very funny about their colors. After they'd actually printed the covers for *Thing*, Alison Lester, the illustrator, looked at it and said, "That's not the green I had in my painting." So all these covers had to be sent back and printed again. I really couldn't tell the difference, but it wasn't her green.

Thing, the story of a girl and her pet stegosaurus, has actually been a very successful book. There's a German edition. At the moment, it's gone into Japanese. And it's been televised in cartoon form by the Australian Children's Television Foundation. I wrote a sequel to that book called *Thingnapped.*

Picture books are always fun to do. Unfortunately, with the recession on in Australia at the moment, they're having terrible trouble selling them. But working with them is just beautiful.

Artists can run into all sorts of trouble. They put jokes of their own into it. One artist used her own Dalmatian and her daughter as models. The little girl has a habit of pretending to peel the spots off the dog and put them all over her face. So the artist put that in.

After the book was published, I got this letter from a school, I think in Sydney, saying "Do you realize on page such and such your artist has drawn a filthy, pornographic picture?" And I looked at it again and I read on in the letter. "She's got a girl lifting out feces from underneath the dog's tail and eating it." I read it to the artist and she was horrified. She said, "Never again will I put an ambiguous shape in a picture."

So I wrote back to the kids and said "You dirty-minded little horrors." I thought that was so funny because looking at it, that is just what kids would think.

I guess in America kids really loved the Penny Pollard books. I think Penny travels well. Penny Pollard is a series of five books. Actually, I wrote it as one book and from that first book, it grew into a series. The artwork in there is lovely.

Ann James designed the first one as an old exercise book. She uses black-and-white format and little drawings a kid might have done. I do like all the drawings because they look like drawings kids actually do fiddle around with a bit in their exercise books when they're bored.

Children just adore it because they all think Penny's real. I've got letters from boys and girls in the Northern Territory who say, "Has Penny Pollard got a girlfriend and would she like to stay at my sheep station when she comes up north?" So it's been a very good story.

Ann's a very, very clever artist. She can look at the book and create such wonderful illustrations because she's got such a peculiar, dotty, very strange way of looking at things that always comes along with this lovely, zany sense of humor.

In *Penny Pollard in Print*, Penny has to be a bridesmaid. Ann has put all these witty details in there—you can see at the bridal table that Penny's shoes are all kicked off. This is really nice.

For *Penny Pollard's Letters* she actually made this leather writing case and photographed it as a back cover.

When I went to England, I took Penny with me and turned the experience into a book, *Penny Pollard's Passport*. Wherever I'd go I'd see things she'd collect. Like her feet were cold on the bus so she used emu socks. Really nice little things.

I did a *Penny Pollard's Guide to Modern Manners*. The editor from Oxford University Press came to me and said that a lot of children are growing up and they've got no idea when they go to the restaurant what to do with the cutlery. And often kids have no idea how to react if one of their friend's parents dies. I thought there was a need for a book like this with a child writing and giving advice. It's actually been quite good, and it's served its purpose.

Unfortunately, I was planning to do a series of 20 Penny Pollard books, but I've lost her. *Australian Women's Weekly* wanted me to do a regular column about Penny. I did it for about a year, and I think I killed off Penny because I got so sick of her. I can't get her back. It's sort of sad. I really cannot get her back. I've sat down and tried. I think she's gone for good.

The newest book I've got out is *Dresses of Red and Gold*, part of a quartet of books set in the '40s. I think that was a very gentle time to be growing up in Australia. The first one in the series is *All in the Blue Unclouded Weather* and that got a lovely review in the *Horn Book Magazine,* which I'm very pleased about.

I wanted to get the same artist to do the cover for the second one, but she was over-committed. So we had to get an artist whose style would fit in with that. I think she's done quite a good job. It's rather a nice cover. The colors give it a very autumny kind of feel.

Boss of the Pool has been quite a good one. It's been made into a stage play with a real swimming pool. The story is about a kid named Shelley, who's very nervous about physically and mentally handicapped people. Her mother gets a job as a nursing assistant, and every night she has to go work at this hostel for physically and mentally handicapped people. In spite of herself, Shelley gets involved and ends up teaching Ben, who is full-grown but mentally a toddler, to swim.

Hating Alison Ashley is a book kids really seem to like. It's been made into a stage play that has been produced in some of the schools around here. Kids have a wonderful time because they really relate to the kids in the story and what happens to them. Every school has a bad boy like Barry Hollis. So they inevitably pick the Barry Hollis to play a part in it. It really has traveled because I think kids are the same all over the world.

I get some wonderful letters from kids in America about *Hating Alison Ashley*. One girl wanted a copy and sent some American money over and wanted to pay for it. It was actually very sweet of her. I think it's in some book club now.

Halfway Across the Galaxy and Turn Left has been made into a television series with 24 half-hour segments. It's not on air yet, here. Actually, it's been shown in Germany. Germany put up half the money. It's having quite a good success in Germany at the moment, mainly because one of their top young actresses plays one of the girls in it.

They've done an incredible job of it. They had a very good budget, and they had some of Australia's top actors in it. They found this little girl who's never acted before and she's a natural. I went down to watch them rehearse. The whole thing has come together and the settings and the costumes are just beautiful. It's really exciting when you see something like this being made for television. We're hoping it all just translates well.

Girls seem to like *Laurie Loved Me Best,* but, unfortunately, it got slighted by a very powerful reviewer over here. And I was very cross about it because I knew kids would like it. Apparently, for some reason, it's very popular in England. It's used as a class book over there. It's got a very Englishy kind of feel to the cover and format of it.

The Enemies has had an American publisher actually pick it up, but they made me translate it. Actually, they translated it into American. It was quite funny, because I noticed mums become moms. I think I had vegemite in it. When it was translated into American, vegemite became peanut butter, which wasn't too far off. But when the book was translated into Japanese, vegemite became chocolate pudding or something like that. Some things travel. Some things don't.

I have reservations about translating Australian books into American or English idiom. I think publishers are underestimating the children over there. Australian kids cope quite well with American terms that aren't common here, like homeroom, which we didn't know. Kids read it and they get the sense of it.

I think by changing it into your own idiom, you're denying them a chance to learn other terminology. Now all kids know what an anorak is from reading English books.

I think it's actually quite a mistake, but I don't know how you stop it, because it's so thoroughly entrenched. You do find that attitude sometimes in reviews. The review will be qualified "This book is good but American children might have trouble coping with the Australianisms."

I think, what a lot of rubbish. Those people are underestimating the intelligence of children. That's not the case, it really isn't. Kids can cope with a lot more than we give them credit for.

Australian books are actually very slow to get published in the United States. If we can get into that big market over there, we're very lucky. Because you have so many good writers of your own, you don't need any other country's. That's my view anyhow. I just feel to get into another country you're very, very lucky.

I think it's terrific if kids can read a lot of books from other countries. The books are one way to show children distance and barriers that shouldn't be there. I always get a tremendous stroke when I get letters from children in other countries. It's quite strange to launch your book out and see where it's going to head.

I had a whole lot of letters in Spanish the other day, because *Came Back to Show You I Could Fly* has been translated into Spanish. It was nice to see all these letters from kids in a Spanish high school Evidently, they got something out of the book and that's the way it should be.

I think that's one of the best things about being a children's writer, you get lovely letters from your readers. It's just really great. I especially like the ones I get from the Outback—the kids that sort of can't get to school because they're isolated. One little boy wrote: "I hated to read but I found one of your books and it had me in it so I might read another book." So that's what makes all the hours at the typewriter worthwhile.

I get so many wonderful letters that I save them all and turned some into a book called *Dear Robin*. The letters are absolutely gorgeous. Here's what some of them say. "I was going to be a writer. Now I've found out surgeons make a lot more money." "How do you know children's words?" "Do you read your own books?" "Have you and Judy Blume got any relations?" Kids always think all the writers know each other. And I get, "Could you give me Judy Blume's address?"

I met Judy Blume when she was here in 1980—lovely lady, very nice. There's one of her books the educational department up in Sydney got very upset about, because it had some sexual references in it. They said, "No, we're not going to have the book in schools. We'll have lots of complaints from parents and everything." I read the book, and it was quite innocuous for the age group.

You're up against it writing for children. I've had my books banned in one school—mainly because I said "piss off." You've only got to sit here and hear all these kids who go to school down there and every second child is saying it. I got a very indignant letter from the head mistress saying

not only had she burned my book, but she expected me to
send her a copy of a more wholesome book to replace it.

And I wrote back in a very pompous letter saying,
"Well, in that case, you'd have to burn Chaucer and
Shakespeare and go through the Bible and black out a whole
lot of passages."

And I think it's a very silly view—kids don't learn
language like that from a book for a start. They learn from
what is said, not from reading. Any child is intelligent
enough to realize that because a character speaks a certain
way doesn't give them license to do it.

I just felt she was attacking my integrity because there's
no way I'd try to corrupt children or teach them wrong
things. I'm always trying to give them some positive insights
because I think that's what they need.

I always try to make my books with a very positive
ending, because kids now read a heck of a lot of doom and
gloom. I'm sick of those books that are set in the future—
everything has been wiped out and they're living in caves.
I'm just sick of those books—there are so many of them
around.

Often I get asked, "When are you going to write a proper
book?" The question just makes me jump up and down with
rage. Every time someone asks me that, I think, "What
constitutes a proper book?"

When I see adults at the library getting all the novels and
other adult books, I feel like saying, move down to the other
end with the children's books. That's where it's all at. It
really is. It is just so patronizing that people who haven't
read many children's books see all children's writing as
Cinderella. It really is heart-breaking.

Some of the loveliest writing in the world has been done
for children. That's not just true of our books today with all
the brilliant writers we've got now. Wonderful writing has
always been done for children.

Something I read recently stuck in my mind because it's
quite true. "If you're lucky enough to have a child in the
house, you have a captive fairy. If you find the right
combination of words you will make that captive fairy emit
beautiful peals of silvery laughter."

You take being a parent or working with kids for granted, but really you're a very privileged person. I think one of the most endearing things about the human race is this capacity to delight and entertain children. It seems to be in every single race and in the most horrible periods in history.

I remember while the Gulf War was on, I saw a film clip of this big tough GI playing baseball with a lot of little Iraqi refugee children. I find it very touching this instinct to entertain and nurture the young.

Kids have always intrigued me. I think they understand very well that the world is a very strange place indeed. Adults try to rationalize it. It's just a very, very strange place. No one knows why we're here, what we're doing here. Kids seem to understand that; they know there's a mystery about it. They know it's spooky.

When you watch a child seeing things, you see things in a new way. Think of watching a kid seeing something new for the first time. Something like a soap bubble—wondering where this lovely magical thing comes from. I'm seeing this now because I have four small grandchildren. So I'm going through it all again—it's wonderful.

Kids actually do beautiful writing because they're seeing things for the first time. The best piece of literature I ever read in my life was written by an eight year old. It's got plot, it's got mood and economy of words. I thought it was perfect. I wish I had written it.

It was "Plip Plop Plat. What was that? Four fat raindrops on my hat." I think it's exquisite.

I think everyone who is into writing knows very early on that that's what they're going to be. I knew from the age of five. I can remember getting into terrible trouble because I used to steal my mother's writing paper.

Looking back, I was actually a very gloomy child. I liked gloomy things. I used to love the story of *Jane Eyre* when she was at a terrible boarding school. I used to hang around the cemetery and lie on the graves pretending to be dead. I thought it was quite normal, but apparently it wasn't.

I haven't got very much from my childhood because we got burned out. But I do have a letter I wrote when I was 10.

My sister sent it back to me. I had written to her when she was away during the war.

It says: "Dear Dawn, Sandra is in hospital with a broken leg." Starts off very cheerfully—"Dad had been giving her a ride on the pony on the other side of the road and he told her to run across home while he talked to a man in a car. He didn't think to see if a car was coming the other way and a car was coming. It hit Sandy just as she got to the side of the road and knocked her unconscious. Her face was bleeding and her leg was covered with mud. The man took her to hospital where she was X-rayed and her leg put in plaster. Rita Baker's baby died a week ago. Our kittens died a month before and a car overturned yesterday but we don't know whose it was. Love from Robin."

I thought these were lovely pieces of news. She saved the letter because she thought it was so depressing.

I'd lie awake at night telling myself stories. I honestly thought that was what every person did. I got quite a shock when I started school and realized I was the odd one out. I really thought that's what everyone in the world was meant to be doing, telling themselves stories and writing.

I had actually a very advantaged childhood—there were nine of us living in the country. Father was trying to get the farm going. He had been wounded in the Great War, and he couldn't work and we were very, very poor. Looking back it was a very good background for a writer.

Of course, we had no toys or anything else. It was almost like being a Trappist monk, where they used to take vows of silence. Probably they don't anymore, and they wear jeans and call each other Bill or something.

I think those vows of silence serve a purpose—to clear the decks for action, which is developing your spiritual life. And I had a childhood like that because we had no distractions. We learned how to look at rocks and stones. I used to spend hours out at the river staring at all those fish in the river. It was actually very, very good training for a writer.

PETER GOULDTHORPE

Peter Gouldthorpe is an illustrator whose book *Hist!* was nominated by the Australia Book Council for Picture Book of the Year in 1992. He found art school a stifling experience: abstract expressionism was the only acceptable style there. You'll not find one typical Peter Gouldthorpe style. His books reflect his eclectic talents. He told us how he chose illustration styles to complement and enhance each story. Peter spoke with us just after giving an illustrated talk to an attentive group of school children at Dromkeen, which houses the outstanding collection of Australian children's literature.

I'm never sure where to begin with a group of adults. I thought maybe I'd do it a little differently from the way I normally talk to kids—kids are easily entertained. Probably you would like a few insights into the way I think and work, so I'm going to offer you a bit of that.

Although I actually began as an artist, now I think of myself much more as an illustrator. When I started illustrating, I started really with an artist's perspective. I'd like to tell you how that's changed over the years, slowly but surely.

I studied art for two years before I dropped out of art school. Art school was a very uncreative place dedicated to fostering fashion instead of diversity. I wanted to paint landscapes and people. But all the art school offered was abstract expressionism. I would paint a landscape and put it in an exhibition. People would buy it. And the art world would say, "Yeah, but it's not modern art."

Half the fun of being an illustrator is to get inside the story, to discover the style and medium that will enhance the story. I don't want to be trapped in one box, so I have gone out of my way to invent styles.

Jonah and the Manly Ferry was my first book and it was done with linocuts. I'm not using the linocut as a block,

123

the way you usually visualize it. I'm really using the linocut as a leadlight—as if it were the leading in a leadlight window.

I chose linocuts for *Jonah* because I have a thing for leadlight windows—the notion that color comes through leadlights so beautifully. You see red in a leadlight window, when there's light shining through it, and it's like no other red. I thought those leadlight colors would actually represent the colors of Sydney Harbour, where the story is set.

I was there the other day, and it was a beautiful Sydney Harbour-type day. I now live in Tasmania, but I grew up in Sydney. To me as a child, Sydney Harbour was filled with light and color and excitement. In *Jonah and the Manly Ferry,* I wanted to show the way I saw it as a child.

Also, I remember as a child the excitement of color. I remember when I looked at picture books that were really colorful, somehow or other I was almost drawn into the page—it almost overwhelmed me. Somehow I'd go from here—looking at the book—to being in the book. And color seemed to play a part in that for me.

So with those two ideas in mind, I set about illustrating this book, which has great big rectangular pictures, almost like paintings. In fact, as I worked on the illustrations, I would pin the illustrations on the wall rather the same way I would when I would do a painting or a drawing. I would pin that on the wall and step back and look at the illustrations from a distance.

But you don't look at books from halfway across a room. So I was making a big mistake right from the start. Perhaps the only reason that a book like this really succeeded was because I put in lots and lots of detail.

I felt that detail was very important. I really wanted to show all the things that go on in the harbor and a lot of incidentals. So when they're going for the ferry, the reader sees the Harbour Bridge and different ferries and the Circular Quay, the buskers, and the shops and the window where you buy the tickets and the people coming and going and all that sort of thing. All these little details I think made this book a success. Without them, it probably wouldn't have worked.

The story is one level of the book and maybe, intuitively, by putting in so many details, I was doing something I didn't fully understand at the time to add another level.

Jonah and the Manly Ferry was my first book, so I was heavily edited. The story is not something I'm all that proud of; I don't really claim it as my own. The final came back rather edited, despite the fact we'd edited it and edited it along the way.

You can see pages where the text and my illustrations just don't fit. I'd done some illustration to accommodate what I assumed would be a page of text and the *page* came out to be a fairly large paragraph, which didn't fill in the space I'd left for it.

Another restriction I hadn't learned to live with was the number of pages in a book. I know most picture books are 32 pages. This one is actually 24 pages.

I was disappointed about the illustrations from the initial draft that were left out. In one case, I had an illustration of the little boy telling the sailor what he had just seen. The next illustration shows the sailor going to tell the captain what he had seen. On one page the picture was rocking left and on the facing page the picture was rocking right to show the movement of the ship.

I wanted to show the rescue scene in much more detail. And yet one page is all we get to see of the rescue. I felt it just wasn't enough. But the publisher decided, for whatever reason, that these all should be just single images. So some of the excitement I tried to create in my initial draft isn't there in the finished book. And because it got cut down to 24 pages, it was too short, rather than too long.

My next book was *Don't Get Burnt*. The real reason for this book is right here in the subtitle, *The Great Australian Day at the Beach*. It was the author's deliberate intention to make it a day at an *Australian* beach. The story in this is very light.

A lot of people said to me when I started working on this, "You're crazy. That's a lousy story. Why do you want to illustrate it?"

I wanted to do it because all the books I've seen to date that deal with the beach only ever show the English view of going to the beach. The people still have their shoes and socks on and if they get wet, that's a bonus.

In Australia we have an entirely different view of the beach. Summer holidays were six weeks long. As kids, many of us would go to the beach for the entire day—days at a time. We'd come home with sand in everything and salt all over us and nearly always burned. Except by the end of summer we were brown as berries.

And that's exactly what the author had in mind when he wrote the story. Most kids get to write about their day at the beach when they come back from summer holidays. The teacher, who is trying desperately to get everything organized, says, "Look kids, I want you to write about your holidays or the day at the beach or something." So *Don't Get Burnt* is told in that droll kind of fashion.

Illustrations for *Don't Get Burnt* were done in watercolor and colored pencils. I've started to move with the book a bit more in the ebb and the flow of the text, and I'm playing around with the pictures much more. I'm starting to incorporate the text within the pictures, being a bit more playful about the arrangement. I really had fun doing this.

Rather belatedly I learned an important idea about illustrations. One of my publishers once said to me, "Maurice Sendak says that we shouldn't illustrate the text." And I scratched my head and thought, "Well, what else can illustrators do, if not the text?"

Then I began to realize the illustrator could create a subtext with the pictures.

In this picture from *Don't Get Burnt,* we've got a fairly bland sentence: "He got a good position in the front to see the finish of the iron man race."

So, of course, I've illustrated those words fairly faithfully. But when I drew the finished art for that drawing, I was bored, to say the least, by the result. Finally, I came up with what was, in fact, an image for that bland sentence that adds something to the text.

If I use this illustration with school kids that I talk to, sometimes I'll say, "Who thinks the guy in white won the race?" About half will put up their hands.

Then I'll ask, "Who thinks the guy in blue won the race?" And the other half will put up their hands. Then I offer them a third option, which is, "Who thinks that it was a tie?"

And some of them haven't thought of that. So there's a third option. If I sort of stand back, the kids will all start arguing and talking about why they think that one person or the other won the race.

So it slowly dawned on me that the illustrator can, in fact, illustrate the words that tangentially start to create another story. I'd just become a little bit more aware of that. So when my next book came along, I was really stunned to find I was firing a bit as an illustrator.

My book *Walking to School* has actually been published in America and, sad to say, it was remaindered here. In one American magazine, they actually used an illustration from *Walking to School* on the back of the cover that had the editor's choice, alongside the Caldecott Medal winner. I thought that was pretty good. Despite the accolades it received in America, it didn't do well there either.

When I chose to do *Walking to School*, I hadn't done a book for a while. I'd been hanging back waiting for something perfect to come my way and it didn't. I'm also an illustrator and a full-time parent. I do most of the housework and the washing and all the rest of it. My wife's the real breadwinner. So I was a bit preoccupied with all of that at the time.

Then along came the opportunity to do this book. Our daughter was about eight by that stage, and she was facing the notion of walking to school. Well, I was really the one facing that, because I was nervous about her walking to school. She didn't seem worried.

Walking to School was a poem which was written about problems of walking to school 60 years or so before. I set it historically, too. I thought it would be a great vehicle for teachers and librarians to talk with kids about how they

walked to school. They could talk about stranger danger—I
don't know if that's a phrase you use in America—and four-
lane highways and all the rest of it.

The dangers for kids today have changed so much. This
seemed a nice vehicle to contrast walking to school now with
walking to school then.

I started to illustrate this book a bit differently from the
previous ones. There's something about this being a poem. I
felt like I couldn't quite use the sledgehammer approach I
had before—loading all the details onto the text. I felt like a
poem was something that lived in your heart, as well as your
head, and it needed to be treated more delicately.

Somehow I had to pull away from it as the illustrator and
concentrate much more on the boy and his feelings rather
than working on details and backgrounds and such. In some
of these illustrations I've even cut the background right away
so that we focus on things like his desperate plight with the
bully boys, without being distracted by background details.

The real joy with this for me was probably in the
compositions themselves. I was starting to be more playful
as an illustrator. Coming up with and experimenting with
viewpoints and really starting to play, not just with the
subject, but with the drawing. I played with putting the
drawings together, the composition of the pictures. In one
you see cows bearing down on the boy and you can feel all
that bovine weight heading toward the boy who is running
off the edge of the picture.

These were done with black crayon—those thick wax
crayons. It dawned on me almost a bit latently that I could
actually run my drawings through the photocopier, as I
finish the crayon work. Drawing with a crayon is a fairly
slow and tedious thing to do. Using the photocopier kept me
from getting tight when I got to the coloring-in point. I could
experiment with color since I could always make another
photocopy if this one didn't work out. With a copy I
wouldn't lose my confidence when I started coloring in and
worry that I would ruin a drawing I might have spent two
weeks producing.

I accidentally discovered something when I photocopied
pictures before I sent them to the publisher. I noticed a

certain graininess. There is a grain in the original picture, but when I photocopied, my picture became like an aquatint.

An aquatint is an etching process. If you think of the prints of Goya and the tone that he uses, the speckledy tone that he gets, that's an aquatint. The photocopier produced something like an aquatint for me without all the acids and resins and all the rest that goes into it.

I was beginning to break out of the rectangle in the pictures in *Walking to School,* but I broke free of the rectangle completely in my next book, *Sheep Dogs.* The shapes, sometimes more blatantly and sometimes less blatantly, relate to what is going on in the story. When they're waiting for the school bus, the picture is the shape of the bus.

My wife is actually a primary school teacher. She had children who couldn't read and found books a bit threatening. So, rather nobly, I conceived this idea to put a picture within a shape. Here was a book where the teacher could say, "Let's flip through the pictures and look at the shapes. See if you can guess what the shapes are. Forget about the words. Just enjoy the pictures."

As I say, that's my noble aim for doing that. It was really a bit of a leap in the dark doing this, because I didn't know how it would look in the book. The text was put on in a rather bland way, I thought.

Nevertheless, I ended up sticking with doing pictures in a shape for another reason. It fit so well with the very thing that the dogs are doing, which is disguising themselves. The story is about two dogs who disguise themselves as sheep.

They're pets on this farm, and they cause the farmer all sorts of upsets. You see one dog on the cover shredding the farmer's gumboots, and the farmer is coming along trying to rescue it. When they overhear the farmer planning to get a sheep dog, they feel threatened. They are afraid they will be replaced. So they go to the shearing shed, roll in tar and roll in wool to disguise themselves as sheep. The pictures reflect the disguise.

A rather unkind review of my next book *Hist!* said how dare you torture children again with this. *Hist!* is a poem that almost passed into my family folklore. My mother actually did this poem in school. I did this poem in school. My brothers and sisters did this poem in school. If we would go out somewhere at night or if we were walking in the dark, one or the other of us would start rattling off a little bit of verse.

A generation later I was crossing a park with my daughter. We'd had a fireworks evening and so there was smoke wafting through the trees and it was a nice eerie light. I started to recite, and she said, "Don't Dad, that's terrible. It's scaring me." A bit further on she said, "Do you know any more?"

I thought maybe I could hunt this poem out and illustrate it. In fact, I didn't know C. J. Dennis had written it. C. J. Dennis was quite a famous writer for adults. I didn't realize he'd written so much for kids until I started to research this.

I had to go into libraries and say, "Hist, hark, the night is very dark," and the librarians all looked at me and thought, "Oh, we've got a looney. Should we press the trouble button or what?"

Finally a librarian, who was very knowledgeable, pointed over to the shelves and said, "C. J. Dennis, you'll find him over there."

When I found the poem, I was incredibly disappointed. It wasn't what I remembered. It wasn't the frightening, wonderfully imaginative poem I remembered. In fact, there are only three things that constitute a real fright in the book. I was very tempted to put down my tools and forget about the poem, but it kept on haunting me.

As I said, I'm a slow thinker. Finally, I realized *Hist!* had lived that long in my mind because it sets off the imagination. It really is a poem about what you imagine in the dark, not about what actually happens in the dark.

As soon as I had worked that out for myself, I decided that I had to show another level to the poem. And that is why the dark borders with scary silhouettes in this were born—to show the dark and what you are imagining in the dark.

As soon as I had that idea, the whole thing fell in place and worked like clockwork. I was really nervous about taking on another linocut book, but it just seemed like the right medium for this particular poem about night and things scary.

I could have drawn most of these things, but when you cut into wood or into lino, you get a slightly rougher edge. You can't quite cut into it as neatly as you can draw it, so the thing gets slightly, and I use this word in inverted commas—so it gets this "primitive" feel to it.

The reviewer who didn't like *Hist!* particularly criticized the borders. If she'd seen and talked to any teacher or librarian or parent of young children, she'd have realized the borders work well with children. She was sort of saying it ruined the subtlety of the poem. Well, that's her opinion and she's entitled to it. But I suspect if she knew more about how books worked, she wouldn't have said it.

I don't think she likes children's books. In fact, I don't think she likes children. She called my friend and fellow illustrator, Alison Lester, the Laura Ashley of book illustrators. Laura Ashley is actually pretty fabric. But that was meant to be a put down.

That is the sort of thing I consider uninformed criticism. In one sentence the reviewer threw a whole lot of things on somebody—it is like throwing mud, then ducking and hiding behind the fence. And the person who's had the mud thrown wants to respond and can't.

It's just unfair to say things like that. I know there's not a lot of space in the newspaper often—but if they're going to make those quick criticisms, they should back them up with real reasons.

I don't think most of the people who reviewed books that were nominated for Children's Book of the Year Awards in 1992 had any base in children's literature. Some of the *Sydney Morning Herald* reviews were by Don Anderson. He is an academic and a journalist, but beyond that I don't think he's got a base in children's literature. He said he wouldn't even want his kids to read one of the books, and he panned a book he'd only read a third of. That's absolutely unforgivable.

I read a story recently that won awards all over the place in adult fiction. I absolutely loathed the book, but I persisted.

It was only the last two pages that tied the entire book together, and I thought that was a fantastic book.

Those negative reviews might just be part of the Australian tall poppy syndrome—I don't know if you have that in America. In Australia, as people get elevated, those in the know like to try to cut them down a little bit. I don't think I'm a tall poppy, yet.

I seldom read the reviews, and when I do, I don't take them too seriously. When I went to art school, I was nicknamed *Nature Boy*, and I think that was the most unkind cut I ever had. It probably drove me away from art school. But it didn't stop me.

You have to have an ego and a thick skin when you're an artist. And so I've survived. I'm not about to let anybody like that really spoil my fun. I enjoy illustrating and you're never going to please all the people all the time.

Most recently I illustrated Paul Jennings' story, *Granddad's Gifts*. I was approached by a company who wanted to turn it into a storybook for schools. This was to be one of the stories in a set of cheap books that they would produce for schools only.

These educational books pay no royalties, so some authors do a quick, second-rate job. But I thought the story deserved the best work I could do. When we finished, Paul asked to have them option it for hardback, and Viking published it as a hardback in September 1992.

I actually met the author on the day I was given the text. Since he lives in Victoria and I live in Tasmania, that was quite a coincidence in itself.

We talked about his story and he looked at my other books. He said, "Oh, yeah, well, that's aw right. But can you do a really realistic style? And can you make it just a little bit weird?"

So I went home and experimented with that. The result wasn't quite what I expected. We talked about having all illustrations in black and white. But most publishers in Australia don't want to know about black and white, despite the fact Chris Van Allsburg has almost carved out his name in black and white and done such a wonderful job, too.

I really would have loved to have done it in black and white. But as I analyzed the story, I realized it hinges on color. The plot has a sort of pivotal point that hinges on a photograph that seemed to me to require color. I really wanted to fix the reader's attention on that point. So I argued with myself and tossed up and sort of voted for color.

I carried out some experiments in order to try and find the right style. Initially, I thought I'd probably do it in oil paints, but it was a bit slow and a bit cumbersome. Eventually I was working in black and white—working in black really—and just using acrylic paint and sort of building it up into a black-and-white photo image to build a base underneath the drawings before I added color.

This particular story is for older readers, and the writer uses a lot of imagery in his story. There were a million images, and I couldn't use them all. Since it was a long story, I couldn't put pictures wherever I wanted to. So I had to take a new tack really.

When I first read it, I speed read to find out what happened next. I didn't want kids to read it that quickly. So I made each page sort of cryptic to force a child to read each page of text.

I think good books and good illustrations are very important. Once books were a child's only escape from reality. Toys were the exclusive realm of the rich. Now every second kid plays with computer games. Every book has to compete with TV and video and all the other things for a kid's attention. So a book really has to offer something special in order for a kid to read it.

JOHN MARSDEN

John Marsden's first young adult novel, *So Much to Tell You*, made a huge impact, winning awards in Australia and the United States and achieving record sales. Mr. Marsden's passion for words and his talent as storyteller make his books difficult to put down and even more difficult to forget. The introduction to *Letters from the Inside* describes his books this way, "Honesty and realism are the hallmarks of his work; he has been widely praised for writing about young people as they really are." Mr. Marsden calls himself a "teacher first, a writer second." When we met him at Dromkeen, he shared creative teaching techniques he uses to encourage his students to write with freshness and originality.

I'd like to start by talking about some of my current passions rather than talking about my books, specifically. I have a great interest in young people and their writing and their language. Perhaps I can cover some of those things and bring in some of my ideas about writing at the same time.

I usually start at workshops by showing kids some of these documents—my scrapbooks. Essentially, the only thing writers seem to have in common is that they all keep scrapbooks or notebooks of some kind or other. I'm sure each writer's notebook is different from every other one's. In my notebooks, I collect a lot of experiences, my own and other people's.

I've been keeping scrapbooks for about 10 years, and in that time I've filled just over three. The third is virtually full—there is one blank page somewhere, I think in the recipe section there in the back. If you want a good recipe for carrot salad with sultanas and pecans, you'll find one there.

I got a bit frustrated 10 or so years ago when I realized just how much of this material was slipping straight down deep in memory and getting lost in there somewhere. So I started jotting things down rather than losing them. I still only remember about half the stories I hear, but the ones I do remember, I jot down in here.

135

I also carry a little cutter wherever I go and I'm always cutting stories from newspapers, magazines, and things like that. They're all just funny moments out of life, particularly from children who are wonderful story tellers.

Here's one about a girl in a Melbourne suburb who told me the other day about shopping with her little brother. She gets in the middle of the supermarket and she finally loses her temper with him. He was being completely obnoxious, just a little brat, this little four year old.

Finally, she was just so angry she turned around and grabbed him and spanked him really hard. It was only when she finished that she realized she had the wrong child. I write notes down in very short form: "Girl slaps little brother in supermarket. Wrong kid." There's enough I can look at and remember.

Here's a story a little boy told me. When he was four, his mother bought a $200 bottle of perfume. He saw it sitting on the dressing table in her bedroom and he liked the color of it so much, he drank the whole bottle in one great sweep. He was telling this story to a group of kids and one of them looked at him and said, "Did you smell nice afterwards?" A witty sort of rejoinder, really.

I was in Paris for awhile last year and loved that wonderful cosmopolitan city. I really enjoyed the feeling that I was sort of at the center of the world stage. So much was happening in Europe at that time. The Soviet economy was collapsing and the Yugoslav civil war was building up. It was quite fascinating to feel in the middle of all that activity.

Then I headed back to Australia. I live about an hour or so from Dromkeen in a very tiny place—I don't think you could even call it a town. It has a half dozen houses, a church and a graveyard and that's about all. I don't know that you need much more, really.

First thing I did was buy the local newspaper from the nearest big town, which is Castlemaine. I wanted to see what had been happening in my area while I was away. This was the front page story the week I got home to Australia: a man tried to steal a barbecued chicken from a milk bar in Castlemaine.

The funny thing was down at the bottom, they printed a description of the man in case you wanted to get out and chase him or something. That was the significant event of the week and things were pretty comfortable here in Australia. I really knew I was home again. It's a long way from the world stage here in the country in Australia.

So I'm a great collector of stories. I love stories. I love reading stories. I've always had a weakness for writers who are story tellers. I even enjoy some of the old-fashioned writers, like Nevil Shute and John Buchan, who seem a bit sentimental when we read them now. If they can tell a good story, I'm still going to be sucked in by those stories. Even though they're racist and sexist and sentimental and everything else, the story line is often so strong that it still works for me.

I've always believed writers should start by telling a story. The story is the main thing. Some writers start with a theme or a message. Then they try to construct a story that will convey that message. To me that is going the wrong way round. It seems to me that themes emerge in the natural course of a story.

It struck me a few months ago that in conversation we're always swapping stories. We're natural story tellers. Fifty times a day sometimes we'll be exchanging stories. A kid comes to school and another kid says to him, "You'll never guess what happened on the bus this morning." And they tell each other a story.

When they get home in the afternoon their parents say, "Oh, I've had the worst day." And their parents tell them a story. We're doing it all through our lives. So in the course of an average life, we must hear hundreds of thousands of stories.

I see fiction very simply as a process involving three elements: experience, imagination, and language. Experience and imagination synthesize into the story. Language is the medium for expressing the synthesis of the other two elements.

One of the passions I have when I talk to young people about writing is to encourage them to become aware of how to use those three elements.

The element of imagination is something that we consistently undervalue. It is encouraged more than it used to be in some areas. For instance, I think we've made some progress in creative writing and perhaps in art. But generally, in our daily lives, imagination is not treated with the respect it deserves.

Older students often feel imagination is the province of little kids—that imagination means writing stories about elves and goblins and fairies at the bottom of the garden.

But imagination takes many forms. For one thing, I think it's the ability to get out of your own skin and get into somebody else's and then write from that point of view. To write through somebody else's eyes. To see life as they see it or understand the world from their perspective. That's a very powerful thing to do. And it is certainly a feat of the imagination to be able to actually project yourself into another persona.

That kind of imagination is not just something for a kid. It's good for all people. It encourages empathy, and it breaks down barriers like ignorance and racism and intolerance.

In *The Power and the Glory*, Graham Greene, one of the great writers, wrote just in the middle of a long paragraph, "Hate is always just a failure of the imagination." I thought that was a very profound and very true comment.

If you can imagine yourself in someone else's position, you can't hate them, because you'll understand them. You'll understand why they think the way they do; why they behave the way they do. So hate is always a failure of imagination. And imagination is a pretty powerful and important thing.

Ironically enough, we don't really encourage imagination in the schools. Yet we respect and value it among people who have reached the top of various professions or areas in our society. Adults, who retain that imagination and then put it to good use, are the people who get to the top, whether it be in business or farming or librarianship or hairdressership or whatever their profession may be. The person who is a success is always the one who has a lively and strong imagination.

Imagination also comes into play in language. The student who uses stale and predictable and unadventurous language is really not communicating very effectively. So I always stress to children how very important it is to play around with words, be adventurous with words.

I came across a greeting card the other day that is a perfect example of stereotyped language. You know people buy cards for everything. This is a card for when you want to end a relationship. If you want to get rid of your girlfriend or boyfriend, your husband or wife or partner, then you buy them this. The language is about what you'd expect.

"We've come to the end of a long and beautiful relationship and right now I just want you to know the fact that it is ending takes nothing away from its beauty, its very special meaning. I've loved you, rightly or wrongly, for so many reasons."

Doesn't that make you nauseous? It goes on and on in that vein. And it ends, "I'll always treasure the things we've shared. Deep in my heart tucked away in a special place are memories about this beautiful time and you."

I really feel like writing across it, drop dead, get out of my life or something, which is the real message I suspect.

If you imagine you can pay $2.95, which is the outrageous price I paid for this piece of garbage, and somehow buy a message written by a stranger, which will speak truly on your behalf, you completely misunderstand language.

Not only is the staleness of the language sad. Sadder still are people who presumably believe that buying somebody else's words can somehow convey what's in their hearts. But of course no one else can do that for you.

One of the most powerful things I'm trying to teach kids is that they have to own their own language. You can't rely on somebody else's words to speak for you. Only you can do that.

Language is something you use to express the essence of your personality. You must own your own language so it can speak truly for who you are and the things you hold important in life.

We have a recession in this country and lot of people are out of work. Years ago, actually not many years ago, when we had our last recession, I was employed in a big corporation in the personnel department for just a few weeks.

They wanted someone on a temporary basis to go through thousands of job applications. My job was to take off all the original documents, like certificates and references, and send them back to the applicant before the applications themselves were shredded or burned or whatever.

I found it a very depressing experience because the letters were written in such stale and mundane language. The typical thing was Dear so-and-so, I'm writing to apply for the position advertised in the paper of Saturday the 20th of June. I'm a year 12 student at Kilo High School. My subjects are science, English, math, graphics, and whatever. My interests are cooking, horse riding, chess. This kind of stereotyped language, letter after letter, was just really depressing.

People who use second-hand or third-hand language are not conveying a sense of who they really are. It struck me that we aren't succeeding in teaching young people to use their own language when they write that kind of letter.

Their job applications should be fresh and lively with a strong sense of personal voice to convey a sense of who they are. Applications should be written in language that truly expresses the things they hold important in life so that anyone who reads that letter will feel the energy, the vitality, and the passion of the person who wrote it.

About one in 500 letters I looked at as I was taking off the certificates was like that. Years later I can still remember those few letters because of the sparkle and the energy that really spoke highly of the people who wrote them.

The more we can teach young people to own their own language, to speak for themselves and not to rely on second-hand expressions, the more we're going to help them to communicate, to grow up to avoid the sad lack of communication that many people are finding themselves handicapped by.

The important role language plays in growing up is another aspect that is not often noticed. When we're young, we use the language of our parents. We echo their words and their rhythms and patterns of language. I think part of growing up and maturing and becoming your own person is finding your own language.

Kids from the age of three or four onwards often enjoy using language in very colorful and creative ways. I don't think we should discourage that. It's an important part of the maturing process. It's an important part of finding your own voice.

That is why the language of teenagers should not be discouraged. They are starting to establish themselves with separate identities to their parents. One of the ways they do that is to find words that will speak to them, which their parents won't use and won't even understand most of the time.

There are all kinds of powerful reasons why I think we should continue to encourage young people to develop their own voice. One of the most important gifts we can give them is their own voice and their own skill in language. This will enable them to get them through life in as effective a way as possible.

I was leading a workshop in Tasmania some time ago. While the students were sitting on a cliff looking out over the ocean, I gave them a pretty unimaginative exercise. I just asked them to write about the scene in front of them, to describe it.

One girl wrote about the crystal clear water. I was taken aback, because as I looked out across Bass Strait the water was anything but crystal clear. It was, in fact, a kind of murky gray color, that sort of colorlessness you get on overcast stormy days.

It struck me for the first time just how powerful language programming is. This girl was ignoring the evidence of her own eyes. Her eyes were telling her the water was completely opaque. You couldn't see an inch below the surface. But she was so programmed to use the phrase "crystal clear" in connection with the ocean and water that she used it automatically, actually overriding the evidence of her senses.

Expressions like crystal clear water or sparkling blue ocean or fluffy white clouds are to be discouraged for a number of reasons. One is that they allow second-hand expressions which are not representing the evidence of your own senses and your own experiences.

I have a number of ways to encourage kids to enjoy using their own language. I go through specific exercises to make them aware of what is stale and what is not. For

example, I'll videotape five minutes of a soap opera, just one
segment between commercial breaks. And I'll ask them to
count the number of clichés in five minutes. My personal
record was 25.

Another exercise is to put all these similes on the
board—as cold as...as heavy as...as light as...as slow as....
And I'll ask them to finish the phrases and they all make
comments. Then I tell them to put a line through the clichés
and come up with something original.

One very powerful exercise I use is to take a story, for
example a ghost story. I ask them to tell me all the elements
of the traditional ghost story. For example: What time does
the action always happen? What kind of animals do you
always get in the house? You know, the rats, the spiders, the
cockroaches, whatever. The wolves in the distance. The
cemetery nearby. The dilapidated two-story wooden house
on the top of the hill.

I'm writing all this down on the board. The kids are
throwing this stuff at me, and I cover the board with all the
traditional ghost story elements. Then I get a red pencil and I
scribble it all out and I say, "Everything on this board is now
out of bounds. Your assignment is to write me a ghost story
which has nothing from this board in it."

There's immediate shock. They can't believe it. I can
hear a few of them whispering: "Why did we help him so
much?"

But once they get the idea that they are free to create their
own ghost story, it's a very powerful thing. Suddenly, they
start writing wonderful ghost stories set in the trunk of a car
or a McDonald's hamburger shop or the school library or a
submarine. It's liberating to see this happening.

Another thing I do is to ask them to give me six or eight
adjectives. I write these up on the board. I get fairly
interesting ones like electric. Exploding is always a good one
for kids. Then we might add glass and green.

Then I ask them to give me half a dozen nouns. They
obligingly supply some: maybe school, Michael Jackson,
tree, wombat and a couple more.

Then comes the great moment when I say to them, "Now
which adjectives do you want to combine with which nouns
in order to give something really different and fresh."

It's the most amazing thing—the sense of liberation, the wild excitement that goes through the room. The kids start saying, "Ah, exploding school." "Yeah." "Can you imagine if the school just blows up and there's fragments of school flying all over the district and bits everywhere."

Maybe they will combine glass and wombat. A glass wombat is a wombat that goes around in a glass skin so we can see all its intestines through the skin or something. Or a green Michael Jackson. Maybe he experimented one time too often with coloring agents.

And it's electrifying. We're using language as a liberating experience We're getting new pictures and images by combining two words that have never been combined before.

By simply doing that, we're getting the gist of a story. It's easy to build a story around an exploding school or a green Michael Jackson. These exercises teach them what language can do when they let their minds expand into all kinds of exciting and wonderful dimensions.

They begin to realize they have a choice. They can let language imprison them, which many people do. Or they can use language as a key through which they can explore a whole wonderful new world.

My main object in writing with most kids is to get them to write a lot so they're comfortable with writing. I think quantity is important. You get better at writing by writing. The more they write, the less likely they are to get writer's block or think of writing as agony or torture.

The last thing I want to say about language is that I really like to encourage kids to become aware of language. I want them to notice it, to think about it, to almost soak themselves in language all day, every day, so that they become confident of language. Then they'll become aware of what works and what doesn't, what's effective and what's ineffective.

Again, I refer to my notebooks. I'm a great collector of language, as well as stories. I've collected thousands of examples of good and bad English in my notebooks and I love doing it. Language is a passion for me—it's a great hobby. Everywhere I look I find examples, even in the most unlikely places.

I think our young people often are wonderfully creative and imaginative with language. I clip things like this letter from a magazine for Australian teenagers called *Dolly*. It really is the bible for Australian teenage girls. It has enormous power with teenage girls in our society, and it's quite an interesting read. This is from a letter on the penpal page: "Chow down spacos, drop your macka lot at our wooden box if you want to cool it and show what a .."

I haven't got a clue what it means. I think it's from two teenagers looking for pen friends, but that's about as far as I can get with it. Even though I don't understand it, I love the wildly fresh language that they use.

I like poetry because poets express themselves in language so skillfully. Comedians also make very clever uses of language. Making kids aware of the languages of poets and comedians is a very good way of exposing them to language.

On the other hand, listening to sports commentators and politicians and people like that gives the other side of language, which is often pretty appalling. At the Barcelona Olympics the other day, we had a golden moment from one of the Australian commentators. On Saturday he said that in recent years cycling had gone ahead by leaps and bounds. Strange image.

I had a lot of fun during the Seoul Olympics collecting other appalling statements. For example, one of the diving commentators stated, "Some of the divers had great difficulty getting into the pool." Very serious problem for a diver, you know. I'm quite concerned about them. What he meant was that they were splashing too much as they entered the water and were losing points from the judges.

A commentator got into trouble with metaphors talking about the swimming pool. He said, "Once again today, it was the swimming pool that set the crowd alight." Perhaps the pool was filled with petrol. Strange choice of metaphors.

Then they had a preview of one of the upcoming events, and the commentator said, "In a few moments we hope to see the pole vault over the satellite." Now that would be quite a leap.

In another example, during the 800 meter race, a runner named Juantareno started to challenge the leaders halfway through the race. The commentator, very unfortunately, said, "Now Juantareno opens his legs and really shows his class." Very badly worded. He probably wished he hadn't said that.

Unfortunately, kids who have poor language skills don't recognize false language when they see it. They don't read the fine print and often find themselves in trouble of one kind or another because of that.

We have to encourage young people to improve their language skills. Not only will they communicate better, they also will be less likely to get manipulated and ripped off by people who are using language to con them. People like politicians or advertisers or leaders of those funny little religious sects that want to take over their lives.

We have—I'm sure you have them too—these cans of room freshener you can buy and spray around the house in order to make the house smell like a pine forest or something. I was reading one of these cans in the bathroom one day.

This is what it had written on the side of the can. "Bring the clean natural freshness of the country meadow indoors. Freshen the air in your home with the clean back-to-nature scent as refreshing as the summer grass and fragrant flowers in a country meadow. Warning: inhaling the contents may be harmful."

You really wonder what's going on. These people are using language to manipulate and deceive people into buying something that sounds like it's toxic. And they're using that false, stale language to make it sound attractive. The kind of thing to freshen up your life. But it didn't sound too good to me.

I mentioned earlier what a powerful feat of the imagination it is to project yourself into another persona. As you probably know, I wrote both *So Much to Tell You* and *Letters from the Inside* in the voices of teenage girls. Someone asked me the other day if I could have written the same books with male protagonists. I realized that I couldn't.

I don't feel any constraint about telling a story through the eyes of a teenage girl. I am just as happy to read a book by a female writer writing as a man, as I am to read a book

where the narrator and the author are the same sex. It doesn't
bother me a lot, I must admit. I think part of it is just the
imagination thing.

Choosing the voice of a book is such a complex area.
My choice has something to do with the fact that I feel
females are able to explore their feelings more than males do.
Even though my experience has told me that isn't necessarily
the case, it is the stereotype. Sometimes I think I can write
more comfortably about feelings when I'm writing as a
female.

When Robert Cormier was speaking to a group of 600
people in Sydney, he came up with a phrase which has
haunted me ever since. He said something like, "You think
my books are bleak. You ought to read John Marsden's
Letters from the Inside." I cringed a little at that. His young
adult stories have been held up for years as the ultimate in
bleakness. Now I'm bleak as Cormier and I don't know if
that's good or bad. He also said some very glowing things
about the book, and I really was moved because I've
admired his work for so many years.

Somebody asked me to explain the ending of *Letters
from the Inside*. The ending wrote itself really. I didn't plan
it to end that way. I was halfway through without
consciously knowing how it would end. Suddenly, I knew
how it had to end.

It's a pretty bleak situation, I mean no happy ending. By
the end of Tracy's letters to Mandy, Mandy's brother Steve
is clearly psychopathic. The description of what happened to
Mandy is contained in the last letter. The dreams that Tracy
has are meant to be the main clues, that Steve kills Mandy
and her whole family.

I didn't want to just spatter the last few pages in blood. I
was very uncomfortable writing the second half of the book.
I had pains in my stomach for months running. It was a very
painful experience, and I was not sure whether I'd get
through it or not.

When I realized how it would end, I wanted to be subtle
and understated about it. I didn't want to force something
down kids' throats that they were not necessarily ready for.
So I put in what I thought were enough hints to indicate to

people who were able to cope with it, what happened to Mandy.

In some ways the characters took over and dictated how the book would go. When I realized that, I realized unconsciously it had always been heading that way. Then it struck me, not for the first time, that when we're writing, our conscious mind is writing one story and our unconscious is writing another story we are not aware of, sometimes not until years later.

IVAN SOUTHALL

We met with Ivan Southall at the Healesville Sanctuary, a natural setting for some of Australia's unique animals. Instead of meeting with us all in a group, Mr. Southall chatted with us in groups of three or four as we strolled down winding paths past koalas and wallabies and wombats. He answered our questions about his books and his Australia. He explained how *Ash Road* came from a terrifying personal experience. He mentioned that the carefully plotted *Hills End* took a whole different shape as he wrote. Even so, our visit with him was too brief and informal to be the basis of a chapter. Since Ivan Southall has been a significant force in children's literature, I wanted to include him. When I asked his advice, he suggested I take material from first person accounts already in print and supplement it with answers to my questions. He made a few revisions, mostly to clarify time frames in material I'd selected. I've italicized text that differs from the original. Footnotes follow quoted material to denote the source.

Most of the material in this chapter was written before 1980 and tells the story of a ground-breaking writer, whose books have been loved by children around the world. His comments continue to provide much insight about children's literature, writing, and life.

When I set out to write a lecture—or a book—it is a journey into unknown places; hence, each day has its own tension, its own suspense, its own fortunate or negative consequences. It could be called a disorganized way of life and, for a family man, a hazardous way of life, not knowing what is coming next, not knowing whether any working day will earn wages or turn into a dead loss. This same method—or lack of method—is why I refuse deadlines. Deadlines fill me with panic and empty my brain and conflict with my way of life, of never doing today what I can conceivably delay.

I prefer, simply, to sit and dream across my valley. The large window of my room is as far as I need to go—no pollution out there, none to see or hear or sniff at, just distant mountain peaks and nearer hills, flower farms and forests, and flights of dazzling parrots and cockatoos, snow white, and one morning, three wedge-tailed eagles in company against blue sky and cloud wisps at great height.

We lived without electricity for years, and the water for our taps is caught from the skies off the roof and stored in tanks. If it doesn't rain, we run dry and telephone the volunteer fire brigade. Eager young men in their handsome red truck with brass bells to ring come heavy-footed with a thousand gallons pumped from the creek. If the wind blows, down comes a tree somewhere and the power goes off. Candles are always ready on the shelf, though in the dark they move mysteriously, eluding your grasp. Difficult roads and slopes a little too steep and thousands of acres of densely, darkly timbered temperate rain forest insulate us from the less uncivilized rigors of life. There is a sign on our road, the envy of all Australians not similarly blessed: "Drive Carefully, Lyrebirds Cross."

People say, "What an idyllic place. What a place to work. All that peace." But *now (1973)* I am the father of four and the grandfather *of two.* ...Our chaos is built in. We take it from place to place. No matter where we have lived, the seeds we have planted have come up as kids....

I was born in Australia of third generation Anglo-French stock. Both sides of my family arrived in the Gold Rush— my father's side in 1858, my mother's side in *1853.* That's a long way back. Out of the Channel Islands and out of English counties they sailed 12,000 miles in windjammers and trekked overland, on foot, carrying all they owned in the world on their backs and in wheelbarrows. They lived and worked in the bush; they built their own houses and grew their own food and raised their children and worshipped God—one side without the loss of a child, the other side most disastrously. Oh, the characters that arose; people like Aunt Clara of *Josh.*[1]

Books were not easy to come by when I was a lad. I lived at the fringe of an Australian city where settled suburbs lost definition, and orchards and horse paddocks and bushland began. We had patches on our pants not because it was the "in-thing," but because bare skin would have bloomed otherwise. There were magpies warbling in the morning and kookaburras laughing and long queues of unemployed. We had heard of wireless sets that spoke out loud, but did not own one. Nor did anyone else we knew.

Money went for food, mainly. Public money, what there was of it, went for bridges and roads and drains. There were no libraries for children. I used to walk a mile or so to the library to borrow books for my parents. There wasn't a book in the place for a kid to take away, that anyone told me about. Libraries were for grown-ups, for real people. You know?

Kids read penny comics—full of stories, not pictures—printed in England three months earlier. For us in the antipodes, they were always out of date and out of season; and all the competitions and free privilege offers had long ago closed. No Australian story comic ever lasted more than an issue or two. If it were of Australian origin, everyone supposed—from a century or more of indoctrination—that it would have to be second-rate and because of this conditioning it usually was. Good things came from England, and we expected to accept this as natural. And we did accept it, although everything was different and bore little resemblance to the life we lived at the bottom of the world. Hence, we grew up in a kind of limbo—second-class or third-class English children displaced, out of context, out of tune, deep down doubting the rightness of being where we were.

In the stories we read, English children played in the snow at Christmas time; we had never seen snow and Christmas was a hundred in the shade. English children played soccer; we knew nothing of the game. English children went to boarding schools; what on earth were they? These things would not have mattered if it had been possible to identify—there *is* a universal language greater than these differences, but our stories missed it somehow. The English were always the goodies, the Germans were bad, the Americans were called Yanks and made a lot of noise. Australia never got a mention except as the wilderness to which profligate cousins were sent and out of which lost uncles came. To be Australian in the old British Empire was to be born with a raging inferiority complex (millions of those Australians are alive today), and national life at the adult level was a fierce struggle to prove to the English that at least we could beat them at games. At everything else they were supreme and frequently let us know.

From our English comics we learnt the fundamental truths of life: for instance, people with yellow skins were inscrutable and cunning, people with brown skins were childlike and apt to run amok, people with black skins were savages, but, if tamed, made useful carriers on great expeditions of discovery conducted by Englishmen. It was in order for black people to be pictured without clothes; after all, they didn't know what clothes were. But white nudity was unimaginable. The white body was so sacred it was not proper to look at your own.

Books for children, conceived with artistic integrity and emotional honesty, to help balance this lopsided culture, were not to be found, largely, I suppose, because writers had been formed in the same mold. They were taught not to think but to believe unless by uncommon virtue of intellectual merit or by fortunate accident of birth they were of the elite. Education for the elite functioned in another dimension. Those liberated souls or the brave ones or the honest ones I had not heard of, and they were not to be found among the writers who spoke directly to my generation. The voices of the brave did not get through to the boy or girl sitting up in bed reading the comics of 40 or 50 or more years ago. This is not to imply that the old British world now gone was all bad. For some, as their literature reveals, it was a form of Utopia where they lived and loved in fine houses and exercised their talents at leisure while masses of the population existed in the breadline, their status little better than serfdom. For us, the colonials, despite our inferiority complexes, we did know where we had come from and where we were going; God was in Heaven, the King was on his Throne, and we believed to be British was enough; what greater birthright for anyone could there be?

Did you ever read about a completely believable boy or girl who spoke your language and thought your thoughts and had your problems and experienced your fears and was sometimes bad or stupid or troubled or irritable or sexy or frightened half to death, but could be a nice kid too? If you were an Australian in my day, I am all but certain you could not. If you were an ordinary working-class English child, I am sure you were not much better served *and* for reasons that might have been more disturbing. If you were American, at least you had librarians who liked children, and you did have, even then, wonderful libraries and there were books to borrow, though whether their authors faced life or ran from it or distorted it I am unable to say. I was down underneath, too far away to know, hanging into space by my feet, my brain addled by English super heroes.

Simply from looking at myself as a boy and being aware of effects, I know that the words children read for recreation are of prodigious importance. No matter how you regard this material, as an opportunity to present life to children honestly, without sentimentality or intentional bias, without denying man's humanity or glorifying it or belittling it—or whether you see it as an opportunity to distort or indoctrinate or pervert or enslave—the degree of influence is not something you can put a measure on.

At 14 I was out working full-time and never encountered literature in an atmosphere or situation where it had a chance or I had a chance. As a youth, life was largely work at my trade as a process engraver and attending night school to learn my trade and a frantic spare-time endeavor to appease the fever to write. This was usually done against the clock as if tomorrow I were to die and a million things were to be written down. But a million things were not to be written down except the most trivial absurdities. There was nothing else I knew and my own experience was unsuitable as raw material to draw upon. I had done nothing brave or noble or exciting. I had done nothing but grow up.

I wrote in clichés throughout my youth as I had read throughout my boyhood—of swashbuckling deeds, of nonstop cliff-hanging physical adventure in which the baddies spoke with guttural accents and the savages were black or brown and the cunning heathens were yellow, putting into effect my long and thorough briefing. There was nothing else I knew except the Bible. It, too, was full of super heroes and hostility between races and high and bloodthirsty adventures. Wonderful stories....how incredibly violent everything is. Is the struggle lost at the source before we begin?

My turn came. The boy frightened in a tree, the boy who had never hurt a friend or an enemy with his hands, learned to accept the thunder of flying boat engines in his ears and the warring world of sea and space into which he flew many times. Fear was a part of every day, none more total ththe night he fulfilled and justified his briefing. An explosion of violence in the air and on the Atlantic directed by me. So I was decorated for qualities I admired in others but found wanting in myself. I was given a ribbon to wear under my wings and a silver cross that I have kept along with *Tony's Desert Island* by Enid Leale.

How was it that a coward came to wear a hero's badge? Or had I been misinformed? Was fear not cowardice? Was fear-sickness not cowardly either? The sickness that shook you, that possessed you, that filled you with dread of dying so young, so soon. Were there no such people as the heroes of my life-long indoctrination? Were decorated men scared and ordinary like me? Was being brave—for lack of a better word—something a frightened lad could be?

I did not allow those improper thoughts to be publicly viewed. I held up my head and played the hero with the self-effacing manner best suited to the role, but was never over-reluctant to go without my coat that the glory of my jacket might be seen. True, I was a nice young fellow and didn't boast or brag or grossly misbehave, but I missed a chance to mature before my time. I simply joined the club, but should have baled out from conformity then and there. So for 15 more years in my series of books for boys, I went on perpetuating the myths of my growing up years.

Simon Black was my hero, developed from stories I had written in adolescence. He was the first character I came up with after I set out 27 years ago to take on the world, abandoning my trade and what security it gave me. Cutting adrift. Going it alone.

Simon, this character of mine, was a decorated air force officer, a former flying-boat pilot who had flown in the Battle of the Atlantic, brown-eyed, black-haired, lean, six feet tall, Australian, wholesome, modest, incredibly good, incredibly clever, incredibly brave, incredibly handsome—me! The super me. The same person, of course, as the super you.

Nothing was too difficult for Simon. Getting to Mars back in 1952 might have been tricky, but he made it in the end in a spaceship designed in his spare time between rushing all over the earth solving problems beyond the wit of presidents and kings and the capacity of armies. I didn't write these stories to cash in; they were not an exploitation—my wife and young family quietly starved along with me—nor did I write deliberately to pervert or subvert or indoctrinate or perpetuate the status quo. I thought it was the proper thing and the only thing to do. I was much too busy trying to scrape together a living, working 12 to 15 hours a day, to waste time reading what my contemporaries were writing—and to this moment I still don't know.

Each day, whether the book on hand was for children or for adults, the attitude of mind was the same—a strenuous search for bigger and bolder and more breathtaking deeds. Talk about racking my brain. Talk about stretching every winning post to a mile....

I knew something was wrong, as I had always known, even when I used only to read the stuff, long before I started writing my own. But in my own life, only the war was worth drawing from. Nothing else had happened to me, and I was much too poor and underconfident and insecure to risk earning time on literary experiment—if it had occurred to me....

We lived 32 miles from town, up the mountains, over the top, and down the other side; a pocket ignored by progress and time. Eight and three-quarters acres of bushland and four acres cleared falling from a pot-holed red earth road to a creek in a fern gully several hundred yards below. It was all ours, with a clumsy house of rough-sawn timbers then about 50 years old, and tumble-down outbuildings with harness over rails, and leaning chicken pens though the chickens roosted in trees, and a brooder house, and incubators worked by kerosene and spring-time cultivators and harrows and plows rusting outside....

Behind us the world stretched eastward out of sight across valleys and crests and mountains and sky and cloud. On autumn mornings the sun came up behind a plateau of mist 15 miles wide with such brilliance it was more than eye and spirit could stand. Eucalyptus forest hedged us on the

south, dark and tall and sometimes unnerving. It began a
hundred yards from the house, and I never walked into it.
Shout at it and the echo cracked back. For a while we called
it Echo Farm, but dropped the name. Perhaps it was an
invocation of the wrong kind.

Nothing to write about either, except swashbuckling
stories for boys strenuously invented and documentary
books for adults about larger-than-life adventure arduously
researched, one's own experience not presenting itself as
worth thinking about.

A journalist called, a very good journalist who had
reviewed me twice (1959). I assumed he had come to talk
about my books: I mean, what else? I had written by then
about twenty-five or six and was pleased that he felt they
were worthy of general comment. Later, reading him
through, it seemed he was more interested in the life I led
than in the work I produced. I was surprised and
embarrassed. I was not obsessed by modesty but regarded
myself as an observer, not a doer, as a failure in the practical
sense.

"Where does awakening begin?" I question...whether
anything has an end. I equally doubt that anything has a
beginning. Beginnings and endings are conventions of
language. The specific moment that may be said to be the
birth of an idea or a book or a change is too subtle to be
defined by us. I was taught as a child that Creation is
infinite, neither beginning nor ending, and I am certain at
this point I was not misinformed. Yet there are
opportunities. There are crests of clarity that mark moments
of revelation. There are sources that become apparent when
one is nudged. I have here, for instance, passed in part
across the origins of every book I am happy to own, as well
as a few I would be happy to forget. They are all there; the
characters, the situations, the conflict, the development; all
are there. Within the same words lie originating parts of
other books still to be discovered. Each discovery made and
each book written is part of the last and part of the next.

The major crest of clarity, for me, came one wet Sunday
around 1958. It is as close to a beginning as I know. My
brother and his wife had added their children to ours rushing
about the house. By half-past five I was wearing thin and

out of a head throbbing from noise said to my brother, "What would happen to these kids if we were not here to pick up the bits, say for a year or a month—or even a week? What would happen if they were left?"

"They'd die," he said.

They'd die? Left to fend for themselves in a world without adults, they'd die? Or would they? Super kids would have no problems, but ordinary kids, real kids, a group of kids like ours, as we used to be ourselves, would confront all the wonders of being alive.

Oh, the obvious truth so long in the coming.

Real adventure cannot happen to super heroes; by nature they would have to be insensitive to it; real adventure belongs to us. Being ordinary and inept are acceptable qualities, they give meaning to achievement. There must be contrasts within oneself. One must know weakness to know strength. One must be foolish to be wise. One must be scared to be brave. Adventure is simply experience; the mistakes often enough meaning more than the successes.

I had come to my crest, unexpectedly, on a wet Sunday, or was it a door that fell ajar and I was ready to slip a foot through? "Write it," something said to me, "you know what, boy; get down to it and write it. It's time that kid who thought he was a coward had a book to read."[2]

I don't consider myself any longer to be a storyteller as such. I did once, and made everything fit the story I had in mind. One could call that a form of absolute control, and you can live with it until your patience runs out. Mine ran out *in 1960.* Since then I have found life to be more fascinating than story, and character to be more engrossing than plot. Although I must say, I greatly enjoyed the writing of the three adventure stories...that were to establish me as a serious writer for children and I am not unaware of the continuing readership they enjoy; but they are written, they exist, they do not need to be written again.

All serious writers change, because to them the work itself is more important than expectations imposed or the readership one attracts. You cannot write the same type of book over and over again if you are to grow as a writer, any more than you should read the same type of book over and over again if you are to grow as a reader. Growth, I feel, is

an obligation demanded of both of us—writer and reader.
This is not to deny the need of pauses in our developments.
Life is a climb, but it need not be continuous.

...Seeing anything clearly enough to make words of it:
this I find to be the adventure of the writer's life. The
adventure is when all goes well—but the despair is when
nothing is there—because communicating is what my kind
of writing is about. Once I can see, I can communicate. Once
I communicate, I can see more. The chicken or the egg? I'm
not sure.[3]

One distinguished friend of mine claims that he sees it
all, then puts it down, as Mozart (I am told) used to do. The
magnitude of this intelligence crushes me. Dare I confess
that my creative spirit (if it is to be dignified by the
classification) stretches and strives and struggles? The theme
is always there, dormant or growing imperceptibly since the
dawn of awareness, I guess. The main theme. The lead
theme. The broadest concept of what the book is to be about
in the broadest possible terms, yet sometimes it is so feeble
that it lies all but lost beneath what I finish up with. I am not
meticulous or fussy or impatient at the beginning, even if the
whole thing looks suspiciously like a puff of wind. I find
that building a book is much like building a wall; I manage
best a brick at a time. But there is a difference. The wall you
finish up with often resembles closely the wall you originally
had in mind. The book you finish up with may come as a
staggering surprise.

I choose my characters and to this group of people rarely
add. Those I glimpse first of all usually see me through to
the end. Almost always they grow from reality, from adults I
know pictured as children, or actual children about me now
or known way back. They *do* grow in the book; they
become different in the book. Some are born out of
fragments, fragments of other people, fragments of myself,
and create themselves, create their own lives. Even a name
has generating power, so I know the meanings of names or
can refer to their meanings in appropriate dictionaries. This
can take days, the choosing and naming of characters, with
care, with anticipation, with expectation, even with
excitement.

I select the scene. (These initial steps are deliberate steps.) Is it to happen in a city or a country town, on a mountain, beside the sea, down a hole, up a tree? The pleasurable toying with alternatives. Scene influences character. Bill under tension is different from Bill at ease. Jane on a mountain is not the same as Jane beside the sea. Fascinating.

My book is still a mystery, an unexplored land. It can be anything of a thousand million things; I think one can reasonably say a thousand million books are out there, waiting to be found. But little by little, by luxuriously day-dreaming, I am narrowing the choice down; more often than not drawing closer, unawares to the story that will invite me in this time. Twelve hours a day it might hold me for a week or two weeks or more, just looking for the door, with little to show, but I have learnt not to rush, not to push hard. Better to relax, to enjoy myself, slowly swinging my chair, deleting all uninviting possibilities, or grossly improper ones (that can happen, you know), discarding all stupidities and irrationalities, until the moment is there. Eureka. The door! It opens. A mood, a word, a certainty that from *here* I go on into the unknown, that inexhaustible source of originalities from out of which comes excitement that I wish all could enjoy. The unknown is a word ahead of me all the time; word by word I move out into it, a patient, wondering, questing exploration. A contemplation of the word. This might begin to sound a bit precious. In practice, it is not. It is an adventure.[4]

In 1964/65 I wrote a book about a bush fire, *Ash Road*. I suppose this book has sold more copies than any other I have written; possibly it has influenced more people than any other I have written—in it I have projected *my* Australia in its most terrifying aspect. From all over the world people have written to me asking about heat, about fires, about survival, and the Education Departments in two Australian States asked me to write a textbook on the steps one should take for survival in the event of a major bushfire—because, as they said, I had researched the matter so thoroughly to produce *Ash Road*.

Researched? To write *Ash Road*? This is the gulf that exists between two minds, between the two types of mind. I have stood in the path of a great and horrifying conflagration but never seriously studied a word relating to that kind of experience. So I wrote the textbook, of course. And national fire authorities endorsed it with not a sentence changed. So one does not necessarily produce an unreal world out of abstracts. One does not necessarily mislead people factually by giving shape to one's imaginings. The creative writer can produce reality, a reality that stands up and works in a real world, out of projections, out of identifying with people or situations, out of imaginings. I state this simply as a fact. It is not meant to impress you.

My Australia, this personal, one-man country—the rhyme and reason for so much of my life—is peopled largely by children, particularly by children who are themselves beginning the most exciting journey in the world, the journey into self-awareness and deepening self-discovery. Is there a more breathtaking point of departure in all the drama and panorama of life? And people ask me why I write for children when there is so much else in the world. One needs to have forgotten a lot, I think, to be guilty of a question of that kind. And one needs to be dead, I imagine, to have the gift of seeing into the consciousness of children, and the heart to feel the daily wonder of their emerging world and have no wish or compulsion to share the experience if the capacity happens to be within you....

If one writes for children in the way that I do, it is childhood itself that draws you in, not the lure of story or a desire to beguile the adult librarian or critic. Once it *was* the story that drew me in, as I have said, but not now. Not for years past. My interest now is to explore what I believe to be the most glorious and challenging of all human adventures: growing up. And indirectly this has led me on to a further feeling—that the writer who writes for children must himself go on growing up. Just as the person who works successfully with children must go on growing up, must go on *living* the process. On and on and on, always growing up. Once you accept that you are a man or a woman of adult estate and growing up at least is over—it *is* over, the magic has gone. And I have come close to it, very close to it, through the pressures of life, a few times. And people who have had my interests as a writer genuinely at heart *have*

been telling me for many years that I have written enough
for children, that I have said all I should say to children, that
I should... write my novels of adult experience because I
appear to live a life removed by cosmic distances from the
lives I write about. I think this happens to most serious
writers for children—people tell them they have outgrown
their audience, as if writing for children were a stage or a
phase or a step....

One of the simplest truths of any human experience is
that we have to share it, that we need to share it, that we
must share it, or remain blind to much of its grandeur and
mystery. The sharing of a human experience sharpens our
appreciation of it, and makes the experience itself larger and
richer and electric. Until we share what we have, we often
cannot even see what we have. Until we make the effort to
share, we will not know how much of life we are missing.
Until we deeply love another person, we cannot know what
love we have within us—nor do we learn how bleak it is to
be without it, to be alone....

Have you noticed how frequently films and television
programs of some sensitivity about children simply being
children become "Adult Only" entertainment, "Not suitable
for children." As if truth about childhood is not for children
to know. Once children in pictures or stories cease to be
sentimentalized—and sentimentalizing is simply the process
of dehumanizing—once they become recognizable as real
children in a real world, significant numbers of grown-up
people start getting the prickles. If a novel for children deals
with sexuality in children, which is the most natural thing in
the whole wide world, even stranger things start happening.
One of my books is banned in some areas of my country—in
libraries and schools. A librarian said, though not to me face
to face, "I got to the masturbation scene and as far as I was
concerned that was the end of it. No child I'm responsible
for will get that book from any library of mine." What *am* I
supposed to say to that? That masturbation is natural; that
masturbation is human; that it is probably part of the life of
every human being on the planet? I could say that, couldn't
I? But why should I? There is no masturbation scene in the
book. And I know, because I wrote the thing. It happens
only in the mind of that particular reader who banned my

book because of her own interpretation. Again, I do not
dispute her right to her interpretation—the function of
individual interpretation is one of the exciting mysteries of
the author/reader relationship. I dispute the arbitrary reaction
of withholding the book from others. About the same novel
a school principal wrote to Penguin Books threatening to
institute court proceedings against them and against me for
publishing an obscene work, on the grounds that my account
of a 12-year-old boy rolling in the rain in the wet grass
without his clothes on would pervert innocent children. This
person enclosed a copy of the book with the offending
passages marked in red ink. Every innocent thing, every
living and vital thing, every poetic image in the mind of my
boy, in the mind of the boy I used to be—in red.

There are two conspiracies, I believe, running parallel.
The first is in the grown-up world where certain adults
conspire to conceal from children creative works of any kind
that speak the truth with clarity or beauty about childhood.
The second conspiracy is in the world of childhood itself,
that closed society where children conspire to pull the wool
over the eyes of their elders. The gap between Earth and
Moon is less, I think, than the gap between child and adult
man or woman. Where does the child go? A recurring theme
of mine in lectures and talks is that we misread First
Corinthians 13:11 at our great loss and at great peril, yet few
of the basic truths of scripture are more often taken out of
context or more often used by ourselves against ourselves.
"When I was a child, I spake as a child, I understood as a
child, I thought as a child; but when I became a man—or a
woman—I put away childish things." This theme recurs
because upon it stands my philosophy as a writer. The child
is not my inferior; he is my equal; we are contemporaries.
Not only does my philosophy as a writer stand upon it, but
my philosophy as an adult also. I am all ages together. I do
not perform as a child, but the heart of the child remains
within me; and I will not accept that this is anything other
than man or woman should be.

When the writer who writes for children as I do raises
his eyes, he sees a world without frontiers and people
everywhere sharing with him the world he has discovered
within himself. Grown-ups may discover my world with

surprise. They hold onto my hand and say, "I had no idea that books for children were like this." Well, their surprise is no greater than mine. I had no idea myself that books for children were like this until I wrote them, just as other writers around the world who have charted the courses and done the pathfinding had no idea either. We, too, hang onto each other's hands and say, "I had no idea. It's such a surprise."[5]

In comparatively recent years, children's books, as a generalization, have been dragged up from a trough of superficiality and mediocrity and set in higher places. This drive towards creative excellence for children is an exciting advance of twentieth-century literature, but having started it are some of its originators and prophets and disciples afraid of its destination? Or are we hearing the clankings of the "old guard" ghost that resides in the heart of each of us?

In my own professional life, the need for something better, for a more *productive* role, led me towards a revision of fundamental attitudes and to a degree of fulfillment not only outside the bounds of my capacity as I saw it, but into a kind of wonderland. This fulfillment was based on my earlier awakening—apparent in *Hills End* which I wrote in 1960—to the simple truth that real adventure is not in heroic incident or heroic character, but in the lives of ordinary people. It needed worldwide recognition of *Hills End* to convince me I was not mistaken. Almost six years lie between the conception of that book and the next expression of what it started for me.

Ash Road was a long time in coming and for this the reason was simple enough. In Australia—where the reaction to my work is *most* important to me—*Hills End,* with a few warm exceptions, was received with coolness and self-righteous pomposity.

Hills End, it was said, was not a proper book to give to children. Its ideas, its terror, its "power," its adult logic and its denouement were unacceptable or harmful. It "fell between two stools"—whatever that was supposed to mean. It was neither a book for children nor a book for adults, but simply a writer's self-indulgence. I was then too thin-skinned and underconfident and insecure to take that kind of discouragement, which I read as a personal attack on me.

Initially, *Hills End* was rejected even by my publishers with the comment that it was worth reconstruction. I imagine this was a gentle way of saying it was not worth anything. But Beatrice Davis of Angus & Robertson had second thoughts; she reversed the unanimous decision of her readers that the book was a failure and convinced the Publication Committee to issue it. But two years were to elapse before she was able to get it between covers. Subsequently, the distribution of this book in numerous and on-going editions and in many languages and hundreds of thousands of copies would seem to indicate that children can cope with it. Now there are critics who ask, "Where has the mood gone? Why can't he recapture it?" Revealing not only the shortness of their memories but their ignorance of what a writer is about....

The writer hears an extraordinary amount of drivel about his books perpetrated in the name of review or criticism. There are critics and critics, *of course,* just as there are books and books, and I am not meaning to implant the idea that I am in a state of constant murderous intent when contemplating people who review my work. Well, I don't think I am. There was a time when I seriously considered the comments of certain critics and for a while I believed they had helped constructively to modify some of my less desirable tendencies. I no longer hold this opinion; to heed them was a mistake. They tripped me and contributed to my loss of confidence in my direction as a writer. I no longer read them. The writer must follow his own star. Criticism is for others to read, for their amusement or guidance or instruction. Not for the writer....

How often have I seen bigoted or addle-headed reviewers attack the theme of a book by manipulating the theme to provide the basis of their moral attack against it, and this can be a remarkable feat of gymnastics, verbally and ethically. Then in Australia, notably one could say, there flourishes another kind of sport, riding the Great Australian Hobby Horse, our inferiority complex, which goes down to history very slowly, though everyone professes the desire to be rid of it. When there is nothing else to say and the cut of the author's cloth irritates, they tell him he pinches his plot, whatever that may be, from some other fellow, usually American or English-born. This is the very bottom of the critic's barrel of goodies: in print, declaring the obligation of a fellow-countryman to an overseas influence for themes and services rendered—not because he has the reputation for stealing the property of other writers, but *because* he is a fellow countryman. This is to infer than an Australian, by nature, is incapable of thinking or feeling for himself and cannot possibly take offense no matter how vigorously you defame him. One author I know used to rush outside to slash about a ton of firewood into chips to cool off, while his wife leapt into the car and rushed off to visit friends.

The act of writing and reveling in the making of a book for children to read is a complicated state of mind, in which the technical accomplishments of the adult permit you to play tricks with time and convert the result into words that function on a very subtle wavelength. There is some limitation of vocabulary in the academic sense, but I have yet to encounter difficulties that significantly delayed me. I believe it is possible to depict or portray virtually anything in words regularly used by us all. This does not mean that long words are out; we all enjoy occasionally the use of long or unfamiliar words, particularly those that tease us by their shape and sound.

One thing you will find in good books for children is the imaginative use of an everyday vocabulary without the slightest trace of writing down. It seems to be *impossible* for some writers to achieve. The attitude or state of mind that will produce this kind of writing, as far as I am concerned, is to be found in segments of my childhood which I am able to relive and stretch almost indefinitely. Not the things I did as a child—well, not necessarily—but the things I thought as a child and particularly the way I went about thinking them, the struggle towards an identity which I felt keenly, the acute response I had to experiences of the senses, the anxiety and trembling excitement of the great moments, the elation of the emotional tree-tops, the despair of pain and fear and failure, and the constant shadow of over-riding adult domination. I see nothing beneath the dignity of an adult in reliving any of them. To put away *childish* things is a disaster.

The body of the book I make for children is made up of pieces of me as a child, often imperfectly realized because years and adult experience and the grown-up compulsion to correct or reprove stand in the way. Yet the mark of my own children and of the children of my friends is stamped on many characters...Whether you win or lose as a writer, the struggle to see into the mind of the child that you were is an intellectual adventure far more rewarding—and from my point of view—far more inviting at the present time than other forms of literary experience.

Perhaps it is the intensity of this approach that lies at the root of critical observations that in some of my books hysteria runs a whisker below the surface, principally in *The Fox Hole* and *Finn's Folly* and to a different degree in *Chinaman's Reef Is Ours*. I cannot say that I agree or disagree—I don't know. Where matters of opinion are concerned, I strive not to be dogmatic. I apply this rule as a reviewer when I fulfill that function, and I am equally reluctant to thump the tub about my own books. My opinion of my work changes, usually from the wildest enthusiasm at one point or another to the deepest and most desperate gloom.

To return to the business of hysteria, which intrigues me. From the standpoint of writing, *Finn's Folly* was an all but overwhelming effort written under pressure of indifferent health at a difficult time when our youngest child, retarded and hyperactive and then about seven years of age, was dominating the house and not a minute's real relief could be found. Unlike any other book, *Finn's Folly* drained me. I was exhausted and ill when I finished it, but it was about matters very close to home. The Mongol child in the story was of course a fictional recreation of my own daughter. Max's loss of his parents paralleled the death of my father when I was 14. Yet I saw the death of the parents as my own death, and the children left behind as my own children. The passion that made the book tick, for me, was consuming. And why not? It was my book. I believed I had written a minor masterpiece; it was finished about six months before my doubts became large enough to convince me I was mistaken. Now I am unable to judge it.

The Fox Hole, by contrast, was written joyously in a few weeks. No effort, just fun, though there was beneath it a hidden critical decision. I liked *The Fox Hole* when I finished it and I still do.

Chinaman's Reef was laborious and took about nine determined months. After some initial confusion, I set out to write a parable about war, and *Chinaman's* is how it happened. No apologies. I think it says reasonably well what I meant it to say.

I see no relationship other than the author's name between the three books. Yet these are the books in which I am said to be hysterical, a criticism I do not become aggressively outspoken about. After all, if I am accused of hysteria I am not accused of a crime. This is not the sort of thing that sends me running to the wood heap. But it is worth a comment, because I believe it has a bearing upon what I am trying to achieve as a writer, and it is only upon my intentions that I can speak with any authority.

The writer for children should communicate with children regularly, children other than those who live beside him. He should visit a school certainly once or twice a month to *feel* children around him, and he should be prepared to travel distances—in essential things the children beyond the horizon may be the same as the children in the next room, but there are differences of opportunity and environment and development that can add significantly to the writer's experience. Out of that experience his work may become more relevant.

A few times, instead of my going to schools, schools have driven out to meet me at my home in the bush *(1973),* Kids getting out of buses and swarming from the road up the hill. It's a sight a writer is not likely to forget. A garden full of kids: flowers and trees and kids. A house full of kids all sitting on the floor. You talk to each other for a while. Forty-three want to use the lavatory—and we're on rain water tanks with two-quart septic sewerage. In groups of half-a-dozen they'll come on into the study, faces like a school photograph filling the door.

Or perhaps at a high school in an industrial area ("Culturally deprived kids," the teacher had said, framing her invitation, "they did not believe it when I said you might

come.")—where you have spoken to audiences of junior
form students since 9 a.m. and signed hundreds of
autographs and paused not once, you'll walk wearily to your
car about 3:45 p.m. and want to die. Hoarse and headachy
and stupefied and a 45 mile drive home and someone will tap
on the window glass and you'll wind it down. A fifth former
or a sixth former, a young man looking sheepish, with a
worn copy of *Hills End* in his hand: "Mr. Southall, would
you sign it for me, please?"...

I do not expect any child to read all my books, those that
might be said to begin with *Hills End;* I would be honored,
but I would not expect or hope for it. Kids should get out
into the open fields and come home laden with an armful of
assorted blooms, with all the wonderful things of good
fantasy and recreated history and poetic imagery and high
adventure and nature. If, in the course of a childhood, three
or four Southalls come home in the bunch I am happy. As
for the adults who read me, sympathetically or otherwise, I
hope that one of these days someone will try to see my work
as a whole and not as a collection of parts. I hope that some
will see how this journey of discovery is moving in many
directions, and certain directions are destined from the outset
to be less rewarding than others, but the journey must be
made, nevertheless....[6]

I remain an Australian writer, though it is presently
fashionable to disclaim nationality and plug for
internationality—but I see a writer's origins as critical. His
origins determine what he is and what he sees, and what he
says and how he says it. If he achieves internationality—a
descriptive word, even if I am uneasy about it—I don't
believe it is because he sets out to achieve it. Universality is
a by-product of honesty and genuine emotion. And you can't
buy these things, and you can't manufacture them.

It is not too trite to say that readers respect writers who
are true to themselves, who are true to their origins. The
reader may not be able to say exactly where this shows, but
he will be aware that the book has authority. I hope I am not
asked to define what authority is, because I am unable to do
so. A book has it or doesn't have it and, although history
proves that the world is full of people ready to be deceived,
if not actually proving that the world is full of fools, there's

no real reason why we should join the club ourselves. Perhaps instinct is all we have left; all we can rely on any more. The earth is full of vested interests, of hidden persuaders, of manufacturers, and our children are exposed to their full assault. I would like to say that if a book lacks authority it will die, but too much depends upon the budget set aside for advertising and promotion. There are books that go on selling because publishers go on printing them, because they are business propositions, because they are offered for sale at the right price in the right market place. And very peculiar commodities they are. They kill time, and leave no wound or trace. Therein lies a sermon. How much of life do we allow to be killed without a wound or trace?

That's my story of my Australia—well, the edges of it sketched for you. The detail I leave to you to fill in because the reader brings to each book his own enchanted place, and if the book speaks of human things, we lay our own interpretation and experience over what we read. The reader adds himself to the writer's vision, and the truth either one of us distills out of the same words may be utterly different from the other. We make our own reality out of things that only we can see, writer and reader together, though we may never have met face to face.[7]

Postscript

The circumstances of my private life have changed a great deal since the lectures were written. I have married a second time (Susan, Californian born), I'm 20 years older, live in a different area and for health reasons have not traveled for a number of years. For the same reason, my capacity for work at the desk is much less than it was, though I continue to enjoy it immensely and look forward to it each day. Much of the day, wet or fine, is spent out of doors in the garden, particularly among my fuchsias. Around the mid-1980s I became interested in the hybridizing and development of new varieties of fuchsia. I have a great number presently under test and this year registered the first of them. These 15 varieties will be released during 1994, but I will not be involved in the commercial production or marketing of the plants.

I have been working for about three years on a different kind of novel for mature young persons and interested adults. In a sense, it is probably my "definitive" work, though it may come as a surprise to readers. I imagine the theme is philosophic and expresses my feelings about life and the universe. Presently, it is called *The Young Canute.* The autobiography has been put aside; I experienced difficulty writing in the first person and switched to a third person narrative. It didn't work. I'll come at it again later from another viewpoint.[8]

Whole sections of this chapter have been reprinted with permission from the following sources:
[1] Ivan Southall, "Sources and Responses," a lecture delivered at the Library of Congress on Nov. 12, 1973, and published in the *Quarterly Journal* of the Library of Congress, April 1974. Page 1.
[2] Ivan Southall, "Real Adventure Belongs to Us," May Hill Arbuthnot Honor Lecture, published by the American Library Association in *Top of the News,* June 1974. Pages 375-393. Reprinted with the permission of the Association for Library Service to Children and the Young Adult Library Services Association (50 E. Huron St., Chicago, IL 60611) from *Top of the News,* 1974, Copyright © 1974.
[3] Ivan Southall, "One Man's Australia," chapter two from *One Ocean Touching: Papers from the First Pacific Rim Conference on Children's Literature,* edited by Sheila A. Egoff, Scarecrow Press, Metuchen, NJ, and London, 1976. Page 20.
[4] Ivan Southall, *Journey of Discovery,* Macmillan Publishing Company, a Division of Macmillan, Inc., New York, 1976. Pages 63-64. Reprinted with the permission of Macmillan Publishing Company, A Division of Macmillan, Inc., from *A Journey of Discovery* by Ivan Southall. Copyright © 1975 Ivan Southall.
[5] Ivan Southall, "One Man's Australia." Pages 21-29.
[6] Ivan Southall, *Journey of Discovery.* Pages 14-36.
[7] Ivan Southall, "One Man's Australia." Pages 30-37.
[8] Ivan Southall, letter to Janet Crane Barley, Dec. 14, 1993.

MORE ABOUT THE AUTHORS

This is a partial listing of writings, awards and honors, exhibitions, and further information about authors. Much of the information has come from the authors and some from other sources.

Some lists, despite my research, may be incomplete. In other cases, lists may be intentionally partial. For instance, Margaret Mahy suggested I use an abbreviated list of titles most likely to be of interest to readers of this book. She has had more than 100 titles published; works include picture books, verse, nonfiction, stories published for schools by School Publications Branch, Department of Education, New Zealand, books written especially for emergent readers in Jelly Bean series, collections of stories, junior novels, and novels for older readers. She also has written scripts for Television New Zealand.

The book list from Tessa Duder mentions that her books have been published in the United States, United Kingdom, Australia, and various European and South African translations, but, the list did not specify which books had been published in each country. Some details on her international publication are included in her chapter.

Jeannie Baker, Gavin Bishop, and Peter Gouldthorpe write, as well as illustrate, most books listed under their names. Exceptions, where material was written by someone else, are noted.

JEANNIE BAKER
Writings
Juvenile fiction for various ages
> *Polar.* Written by Elaine Moss. Deutsch, London, 1975; Ashton Scholastic, Sydney; Greenwillow, New York.

Grandfather. Deutsch, London, 1977; Dutton, New York; Israel.

Grandmother. Deutsch, London, 1978; Dutton, New York.

Millicent. Deutsch, London, 1980; Dutton, New York, Hutchinson, Melbourne, and Ashton Scholastic, Sydney.

One Hungry Spider. Deutsch, London, 1982; Dutton, New York; Ashton Scholastic, Sydney.

Home in the Sky. Julia MacRae Books, London and Australia; Greenwillow, New York, 1984.

Where the Forest Meets the Sea. Julia MacRae Books, London and Australia, 1984; Walker Books, England; Greenwillow, and Scholastic, New York; Japan.

Window. Julia MacRae Books, London and Australia, 1991; Red Fox, London; Greenwillow, New York.

Scripts and screenplays
Where the Forest Meets the Sea, a 10-minute animated 35-mm film produced by Film Australia. Director-artist-concept-design-words: Jeannie Baker, 1988.

Special Recognition
Awards and honors
American Library Association Notable Book, *Home in the Sky*, 1984.

Australian Children's Book Council Children's Picture Book of the Year, shortlisted and commended, *Home in the Sky*, 1985.

[British] Library Association Kate Greenaway Medal Shortlist, *Home in the Sky*, 1985.

Visual Arts Book Award, *Home in the Sky*, 1986.

Young Australians Best Book Award Picture Story Books Shortlist, *Home in the Sky*, 1986.

Australian Film Institute Award for Best Australian Animated Film, *Where the Forest Meets the Sea*, 1988.

Boston Globe/Horn Book Magazine Honor Book, United States, *Where the Forest Meets the Sea*, 1988.

Friends of the Earth, Earthworm Book Award, England, Where *the Forest Meets the Sea*, 1988.

Greater Union Yoram Gros Award for Best Australian Animated Film, *Where the Forest Meets the Sea*, 1988.

Parents Magazine Best Picture Books Award, United States, *Where the Forest Meets the Sea*, 1988.

Young Australians Best Book Award (YABBA) Picture Story, *Where the Forest Meets the Sea*, 1988.

International Board of Books for Young People (IBBY) Honor Award for Illustration, *Where the Forest Meets the Sea*, 1990.

Kids Own Australian Literary Awards (KOALA) primary category, *Where the Forest Meets the Sea*, 1990.

Australian Children's Book Council Children's Picture Book of the Year Award, *Window,* 1992.

[British] Library Association Kate Greenaway Medal Shortlist, *Window,* 1992.

Notable Trade Book in the Field of Social Sciences, United States, *Window,* 1992.

Young Australian's Best Book Award Picture Book Section, *Window,* 1992.

Exhibitions

Brettenham House, Waterloo Bridge, London, 1975.

Gallery One, Hobart, 1977.

Bonython Gallery, Adelaide, 1980.

Craft Council of Australia Gallery, Sydney, 1980.

Newcastle Public Gallery, New South Wales, 1980.

Craft Council of Tasmania Gallery, Hobart, 1982.

Dromkeen, Victoria, 1982.

Dromkeen, Victoria, 1983.

Forum Gallery, New York, 1983.

Roslyn Oxley Gallery 9, Sydney, 1983.

Dromkeen, Victoria, 1988.

Lewers Bequest and Penrith Regional Art Gallery, New South Wales, 1988.

National Gallery of Victoria, Melbourne1988.

Noosa Regional Art Gallery, Queensland, 1988.

Roslyn Oxley Gallery 9, Sydney, 1988.

Campbelltown City Bicentennial Art Gallery, New South Wales, 1991.

Lewers Bequest and Penrith Regional Art Gallery, New South Wales, 1991.

Royal Botanic Gardens, Sydney, 1991.

Brisbane City Hall Art Gallery and Museum, 1992.

Dromkeen, Victoria, 1992.

The Museum of Victoria, Melbourne, 1992.

Numerous group exhibits include Albury Regional Art Gallery, Albury; the Australian National Gallery, Canberra; The Royal Academy Summer Exhibition, Portal Gallery, Bond Street, London; Noosa Regional Art Gallery, Noosa; Penrith Regional Art Gallery, Penrith; Robin Gibson Gallery, Hogarth Galleries, Crafts Council of Australia Gallery, and The State Library of New South Wales, Sydney.

Collections
Count Basie, Dromkeen Museum of Children's Literature, James Fairfax, Dr. William Franklin, Bella and Sol Fishko, Island Recording Company, Myron Kunin, Ogilvy, Benson & Mather, The Powerhouse Museum, John Prescott, Private Collections, QANTAS Queensland State Gallery, The State Gallery of Western Australia.

GAVIN BISHOP
Writings
Juvenile fiction for various ages

Mrs. McGinty and the Bizarre Plant. Oxford University Press, Melbourne, Auckland, New York, 1981; Piccolo, London.

The Year of the Yelvertons. Written by Katherine O'Brien, Oxford University Press, Melbourne and Auckland, 1981; Ashton Scholastic, Sydney.

BidiBidi. Oxford University Press, Auckland, 1982.

Mr. Fox. Oxford University Press, Auckland and New York, 1982; Piccolo, London.

Chicken Licken. Oxford University Press, Auckland, Oxford, 1984.

The Horror of Hickory Bay. Oxford University Press, Auckland, Oxford, 1984.

The Hungry Fox. Houghton Mifflin, Boston, 1985.

Mother Hubbard. Oxford University Press, Auckland, 1986.

A Apple Pie. Oxford University Press, Auckland, 1987.

American Reading Book Series illustrations commissioned by D.C. Heath, Boston, 1987.

School Publications commissioned pieces, 1988.

The Three Little Pigs. Scholastic, New York, 1989.

Katarina. Random Century, Auckland, 1990.

Les Trois Petits Cochons. Scholastic, Canada, 1991.

The Lion and the Jackal. Written by Beverly Dietz, Silver Burdett & Ginn, New York, 1991.

Little Red Rocking Hood. written by Jeffrey Leask, Ashton Scholastic, Sydney, 1992.

Hinepau. Ashton Scholastic, Auckland, 1993.

The Wedding of Mistress Fox. North-South Publishing, New York, 1994.

Scripts and screenplays
Terrible Tom, ballet story and design commissioned by the Royal New Zealand Ballet Company, 1986.

Te Maia and the Sea-Devil, ballet story and design commissioned by the Royal New Zealand Ballet Company, 1987.

BidiBidi, scripts for TVNZ. Producer: Max Quinn, 1990.

BidiBidi to the Rescue, scripts for TVNZ. Producer: Jayashree Panjabi, Taylor-Made Productions, 1991.

Special Recognition
Awards and honors,
Esther Glen Medal for illustration, *The Year of the Yelvertons,* 1981.

New Zealand Children's Book of the Year finalist, *Mrs. McGinty and the Bizarre Plant,* 1981.

Russell Clark Medal for illustration, *Mrs. McGinty and the Bizarre Plant,* 1981.

New Zealand Picture Book of the Year finalist, *BidiBidi*, 1982.

Noma Coucours Prize for children's picture book, Japan, *BidiBidi*, 1982.

New Zealand Picture Book of the Year, *Mr. Fox,* 1983.

New Zealand Picture Book of the Year finalist, *Chicken Licken*, 1984.

Premi Catalonia D'Il-lustracio in Barcelona. *Chicken Licken* selected to represent New Zealand, 1984.

New Zealand Picture Book of the Year finalist, *Mother Hubbard*, 1986.

Russell Clark Medal finalist, *A Apple Pie,* 1987.

Russell Clark Medal finalist, *Katarina,* 1991.

Presentations and fellowships
International Expert and Picture Book Artist in training programs in Beijing and Shanghai, China. Organized by the Asian Culture Center for UNESCO for the Publishers' Association of China 1992.

Exhibitions
Seibu Department Store, Tokyo, and Bratislava Biennale, Czechoslovakia, *Mr. Fox*, 1982.

Bratislava Biennale, *The Horror of Hickory Bay,* 1985.

Premi Catalonia D'Il-lustracio, *The Horror of Hickory Bay,* 1986.

Premi Catalonia D'Il'lustracio, *A Apple Pie*, 1987.

McDougall Art Gallery, Christchurch, *Mr. Fox, Chicken Licken, Katarina, and The Horror of Hickory Bay,* 1991.

National Library, Wellington, *Mr. Fox, Chicken Licken, Katarina, and The Horror of Hickory Bay,* 1993.

Judging
New Zealand AIM Children's Book Awards, 1993.

Further Information About the Author
Artists of the Page: Interviews with 29 Children's Book Illustrators from Around the World, by Sylvia and Kenneth Marantz, McFarland & Company, Inc., Jefferson, North Carolina, 1992.

DOROTHY BUTLER
Writings
Juvenile fiction for various ages
The Magpies Said. Dorothy Butler, editor, Kestrel Books, London, 1980.

For Me, Me, Me. Dorothy Butler, editor, Hodder and Stoughton, Sydney, 1985; London.

I Will Build You a House. Dorothy Butler, editor, Hodder and Stoughton, Sydney, 1986; England.

A Bundle of Birds. Reed Methuen, Auckland, 1987; Puffin, Middlesex, England.

Come Back Ginger: A Tale of Old New Zealand. Reed Methuen, Auckland, 1987.

My Brown Bear Barney. Heinemann Reed, New York, 1988; Hodder and Stoughton, London; Greenwillow, New York.

Bears, Bears, Bears. Century Hutchinson, Auckland, 1989.

A Happy Tale. Century Hutchinson, Auckland; The Bodley Head, London; Crocodile Press, New York, 1990.

Lulu. Hodder and Stoughton, London, 1990.

Another Happy Tale. Random Century, Auckland, 1991; Crocodile Press, New York.

Higgledy Piggledy Hobbledy Hoy. Greenwillow, New York, 1991.

By Jingo! A Tale of Old New Zealand, Reed Methuen, Auckland, 1992.

Farmyard Fiasco. Nelson Price Milburn, New Zealand, 1992.

Good Morning, Mrs. Martin. Nelson Price Milburn, New Zealand, 1992.

The Little, Little Man. Nelson Price Milburn, New Zealand, 1992.

Where's Isabella? Random House, Auckland, 1992.

My Brown Bear Barney in Trouble. Greenwillow, New York, 1993.

Nonfiction for adults
Cushla and Her Books. Hodder and Stoughton, London, 1979; Horn Book, Boston; Japan.

Reading Begins at Home. with Marie Clay, Heinemann, Auckland, 1979; England; Heinemann Educational Books, Exeter, New Hampshire.

Babies Need Books. The Bodley Head, London, Penguin, London,1980; Atheneum, New York; Japan.

Five to Eight. The Bodley Head, London, 1985; Japan.

Special Recognition
Awards and honors

The Eleanor Farjeon Award for Contribution to Children's Literature, England, 1979.

American Library Association, *Cushla and Her Books,* 1985.

Children's Literature Association of New Zealand, Inc., Honor for Distinguished Services to New Zealand Children's Literature, 1991.

Officer of the Order of the British Empire (OBE), 1993.

Presentations and fellowships

May Hill Arbuthnot Honor Lecture, United States, 1984.

Anne Carroll Moore Memorial Lecture, New York, 1984.

California Elementary Education Association Teacher Seminars, 1991.

Ezra Jack Keats Lecture, University of Southern Mississippi, 1991.

Margaret Mahy Lecture Award for Distinguished Services to Children's Literature, 1992.

Lectures for foundations, library and reading associations, universities and library schools in Japan, Australia, and the United States.

Further Information About the Author
International Authors and Writers Who's Who.

New Zealand Who's Who.

The Oxford Companion to Children's Literature.

The World Who's Who of Women.

Writers Directory, St. James Press, London.

TESSA DUDER
Writings
Juvenile fiction for various ages
Night Race to Kawau. Oxford University Press, Auckland, 1982; Penguin, London.

Jellybean. Oxford University Press, Auckland and Oxford, 1985; Viking Kestrel, New York, 1986.

Dragons. Shortland Publications, Auckland, 1987.

Play It Again Sam. Shortland Publications, Auckland, 1987.

Simply Messing About in Boats. Shortland Publications, Auckland, 1988.

Alex. Oxford University Press, Auckland, 1987; Oxford, 1988; Houghton Mifflin, Boston, 1989.

Alex in Winter. Oxford University Press, Auckland and Oxford, 1989.

Alessandra—Alex in Rome. Oxford University Press, Auckland and Oxford, 1991.

Songs for Alex. Oxford University Press, Auckland and Oxford, 1992.

Nonfiction
The Book of Auckland. Oxford University Press, Auckland, 1985.

Spirit of Adventture: The Story of New Zealand's Sail Training Ship. Century Hutchinson, Auckland, 1985.

Waitemata—Auckland's Harbor of Sails, Century Hutchinson, Auckland, 1989.

Kawau—the Governor's Gift. Bush Press, Auckland, 1991.

Journey to Olympia—The Story of the Ancient Olympics. Scholastic, New York, 1992.

The Making of Alex: The Movie. Ashton Scholastic, Auckland, 1993.

Scripts and screenplays
Alex, movie script consultant: Tessa Duder. Scriptwriter: Ken Catran. Producers: Tom Parkinson, Isambard Productions, Auckland, and Phil Gerlach, Total Film, Sydney. Released May 1993. Sales to Italy, France, Germany, the United Kingdom, and Canada.

Foreign Rites, written and presented with Martin Baynton, a one-act play for five voices and three hats.

Five Go to the Dogs, written with Martin Baynton, a family entertainment for four writer-actors.

The Runaway, one-act play for classroom performance in *Nearly Seventeen.*

Special Recognition
Awards and honors

Choysa Bursary for Children's Writers, 1985.

American Library Association Notable Book, *Jellybean,* 1986.

New Zealand Children's Book of the Year, *Alex,* 1988.

American Library Association Young Adult List, *In Lane Three, Alex Archer,* 1989.

Esther Glen Medal, *Alex,* 1989.

Queen Elizabeth II Travel Grant for American Convention of International Reading, New Orleans, 1989.

AIM Children's Book of the Year, *Alex in Winter,* 1990.

Esther Glen Medal, *Alex in Winter,* 1990.

New Zealand Commemorative Medal, 1990.

Queen Elizabeth II Arts Council Special Writing Bursary, 1990.

AIM Children's Book of the Year, Third Place, *Alessandra—Alex in Rome,* 1992.

Esther Glen Medal, *Alessandra—Alex in Rome,* 1992.

AIM Children's Book of the Year Senior Fiction, *Alex,* 1993.

Presentations and fellowships

World Congress of International Reading Association speaker on New Zealand children's literature, Stockholm, 1990.

New Zealand Writers' Week speaker, Dunedin, 1991.

South Pacific Convention of the International Reading Association speaker, Rotorua, 1991.

University of Waikato first writer in residence, 1991.

American Convention of International Reading Association speaker, Orlando, 1992.

First National Conference of Australian Children's Book Council, speaker, Sydney, 1992.

Listenere Women's Book Festival touring author, 1992.

Australia-New Zealand Literary Exchange Fellow, 1993.

New Zealand Writers' Week speaker-actor, Dunedin, 1993.

20th National Conference of the New Zealand Reading Association plenary speaker, 1994.

Judging

Bank of New Zealand Short Story Awards and Dominion Times-Mobil Short-Story Awards Young Writers' Sections, 1991.

Goodman Fielder Wattie Book Awards Young Writer's Award category, 1992.

Further Information About the Author
Through the Looking Glass, editor Michael Gifkins, Century Hutchison, Auckland, 1989.

My Father and Me, editor, Penny Hansen, Tandem Press, New Zealand, 1992

BETTY GILDERDALE
Writings
Juvenile fiction for various ages
The Little Yellow Digger. Illustrated by Alan Gilderdale, Ashton Scholastic, Auckland, 1992.

Nonfiction for young people and adults
A Sea Change: 145 Years of New Zealand Junior Fiction. Longman, Auckland, 1982.

Introducing Margaret Mahy. Viking Books, New Zealand, 1987.

Under the Rainbow, an anthology. Bateman, Auckland, 1990.

Introducing 21 New Zealand Children's Writers. Hodder and Stoughton, Auckland, 1991.

Oxford History of New Zealand Literature. Children's Literature Section, Oxford University Press, Auckland, 1991.

Special Recognition
Awards and honors
PEN International Best First Book Award, 1983.

Children's Book of the Year Shortlist, *The Little Yellow Digger,* 1992.

PETER GOULDTHORPE
Writings
Juvenile fiction for various ages
> *Jonah and the Manly Ferry.* Methuen, Sydney 1983.

> *Don't Get Burnt.* Written by Jack Bedson, William Collins, Sydney, 1984.

> *Walking to School.* Written by Ethel Turner, William Collins, Sydney 1988; Orchard Books, New York.

> *Sheep Dogs.* Written by Jack Bedson, Walter McVitty Books, Sydney, 1989.

> *Hist!* Written by C. J. Dennis, Walter McVitty Books, Sydney, 1991.

> *Granddad's Gifts.* Written by Paul Jennings, Viking Books, Melbourne, 1992.

> *First Light.* Written by Gary Crew, Lothian Books, Melbourne, 1993.

Special Recognition
Awards and honors
> Children's Book Council of Australia Children's Book of the Year Honor Book, *Hist!* 1992.

> Children's Book Council of Australia Children's Book of the Year Shortlist, *Granddad's Gifts,* 1993.

ROBIN KLEIN
Writings
Juvenile fiction for various ages
> *The Giraffe in Pepperell Street.* Illustrated by Gill Tomblin, Hodder and Stoughton, Sydney, 1978.

Honored Guest. Illustrated by Margaret Power, Macmillan Orbit Series, Melbourne, 1979; Angus & Robertson Bluegum Series, Sydney.

Sprung! Illustrated by Margaret Power, Rigby Young Magpie Series, Adelaide, 1982.

Thing. Illustrated by Alison Lester, Oxford University Press, Melbourne and Oxford, 1982.

Junk Castle. Illustrated by Rolf Heimann, Oxford University Press, Melbourne, Oxford, and New York, 1983; Germany, Spain.

Oodoolay. Illustrated by Vivienne Goodman, Era Publications, Flinders Park, South Australia, 1983.

Penny Pollard's Diary. Illustrated by Ann James, Oxford University Press, Melbourne and Oxford, 1983; Germany.

People Might Hear You. Penguin, Melbourne and London, 1983; Viking Kestrel, New York.

Brock and the Dragon. Illustrated by Rodney McRae, Hodder and Stoughton, Sydney, 1984; Denmark.

Hating Alison Ashley. Puffin Books, Melbourne, Australia and Middlesex, England, 1984; Puffin Books, New York; Germany, Denmark, Spain.

Penny Pollard's Letters. Illustrated by Ann James, Oxford University Press, Melbourne and Oxford, 1984; Germany.

Ratbags and Rascals. Illustrated by Alison Lester, Dent, Melbourne, 1984; Oxford University Press, Oxford; Houghton Mifflin, Boston.

Thalia the Failure. Illustrated by Rhyll Plant, Ashton Scholastic, Sydney, 1984; United Kingdom edition, *The Broomstick Academy,* Scholastic Publications, England, 1986.

Thingnapped! Illustrated by Alison Lester, Oxford University Press, Melbourne and Oxford, 1984.

The Tomb Comb. Illustrated by Heather Potter, Rigby Young Magpie Series, Adelaide, 1984.

Annabel's Ghost. Thematic pack edited by Ron Thomas, Oxford University Press, Melbourne, 1985.

Battlers (Good for Something, Serve Him Right! You're On Your Own!) Edward Arnold Audiobooks, Australia, 1985.

The Enemies. Illustrated by Noela Young, Angus & Robertson, Sydney, 1985; Denmark, Japan.

Halfway Across the Galaxy and Turn Left. Viking Kestrel, Melbourne and London, 1985; Viking, New York.

Separate Places. Illustrated by Anna Lacis, Kangaroo Press, Australia, 1985.

Snakes and Ladders. Illustrated by Ann James, Dent, Australia; Oxford University Press, Oxford, 1985.

Boss of the Pool. Illustrated by H. Panagopoulos, Omnibus Books, Adelaide, Viking Kestrel, London, 1986.

Games. Illustrated by Melissa Webb, Viking Kestrel, Melbourne, 1986; Germany.

Penny Pollard in Print. Illustrated by Ann James, Oxford University Press, Melbourne, 1986.

The Princess Who Hated It. Illustrated by Maire Smith, Omnibus Books, Adelaide, 1986.

Birk the Berserker. Illustrated by Alison Lester, Omnibus Books, Adelaide, 1987.

Christmas. Illustrated by Kristen Hilliard, Methuen, Sydney, 1987.

Get Lost. Illustrated by June Joubert, Macmillan Southern Cross Series, Sydney, 1987.

I Shot an Arrow. Illustrated by Geoff Hocking, Viking Kestrel, Melbourne, 1987.

The Last Pirate. Illustrated by Rick Armor, Rigby Education, Adelaide, 1987.

The Lonely Hearts Club. Co-author Max Dann, Oxford University Press, Melbourne, 1987; Oxford University Press, New York, 1988.

Parker-Hamilton. Illustrated by Gaston Vanzet, Rigby Education, Adelaide, 1987.

Robin Klein's Crookbook. Illustrated by Kristen Hilliard, Methuen, Sydney, 1987.

Annabel's Party. Illustrated by Mark Payne, Rigby Education, Adelaide, 1988.

Dear Robin. Allen and Unwin, Sydney, 1988.

Into Books: Literature Pack No. 3 (Junk Castle, Penny Pollard's Diary, Penny Pollard's Letters,

Thing, Thingnapped!) Oxford University Press, Melbourne, 1988.

Irritating Irma. Illustrated by Chris Johnston and Rowena Cory, Rigby Education, Adelaide, 1988.

Jane's Mansion. Illustrated by Melissa Webb, Rigby Education, Adelaide, 1988.

The Kidnapping of Clarissa Montgomery. Illustrated by Jane Wallace-Mitchell, Rigby Education, Adelaide, 1988.

Laurie Loved Me Best. Viking Kestrel, Melbourne and London, 1988; Denmark.

Penny Pollard's Passport. Illustrated by Ann James, Oxford University Press, Melbourne, 1988.

Stanley's Smile. Rigby Education, Adelaide, 1988.

Against the Odds. Illustrated by Bill Woods, Viking Kestrel, Melbourne, 1989.

Came Back to Show You I Could Fly. Viking Kestrel, Melbourne, Viking Penguin, New York, 1989; Spain.

The Ghost in Abigail Terrace. Illustrated by Margaret Power, Omnibus Books, Adelaide, 1989.

Penny Pollard's Guide to Modern Manners. Illustrated by Ann James, Oxford University Press, Melbourne, 1989.

Boris and Borsch. Illustrated by Cathy Wilcox, Allen and Unwin, Sydney, 1990.

Tearaways. Viking Penguin, New York, 1990.

All in the Blue Unclouded Weather. Viking Penguin, New York, 1992.

Amy's Bed. Illustrated by Coral Tulloch, Omnibus Books, Adelaide, 1992.

Dresses of Red and Gold. Viking Penguin, New York, 1992.

Seeing Things. Viking Penguin, New York, 1993.

Special Recognition
Awards and honors
Critici in Erba, Special Mention, Bologna Children's Book Fair, *The Giraffe in Pepperell Street,* 1979.

Children's Book Council of Australia Awards Junior Book of the Year Awards, *Thing,* 1983.

Children's Book Council of Australia Book of the Year Awards, Highly Commended, *Penny Pollard's Diary,* 1984.

Children's Book Council of Australia Book of the Year Awards Shortlist, *Junk Castle* and *People Might Hear You,* 1984.

Children's Book Council of Australia Book of the Year Awards Shortlist, *Hating Alison Ashley,* 1985.

Children's Book Council of Australia Book of the Year Awards Shortlist, *The Enemies,* 1986.

Children's Book Council of Australia Book of the Year Awards Shortlist, *Halfway Across the Galaxy and Turn Left,* 1986.

Children's Book Council of Australia Book of the Year Awards Shortlist, *Boss of the Pool,* 1987.

Kids Own Australian Literary Awards (KOALA) Senior Category, *Hating Alison Ashley,* 1987.

West Australian Young Readers' Book Award Special Award, *Hating Alison Ashley,* 1987.

Children's Book Council of Australia Book of the Year Awards Shortlist, *Birk the Berserker,* 1988.

Australian Human Rights Award for Literature Book of the Year, *Came Back to Show You I Could Fly,* 1989.

Children's Book Council Book of the Year Awards for Older Readers, *Came Back to Show You I Could Fly,* 1990.

New South Wales and Victoria Premiers' Awards Shortlist, *Came Back to Show You I Could Fly,* 1990.

Children's Book Council of Australia Book of the Year Awards Honor Book, *Boris and Borsch,* 1991.

Children's Book Award, New South Wales State Literary Awards, *All In the Blue UncloudedWeather,* 1992.

Scripts and screenplays

Thing, televised in cartoon form by Australian Children's Television Foundation, Kaboodle Series, 1987.

Penny Pollard's Diary, televised by Australian Children's Television Foundation, Kaboodle Series, 1987.

Hating Alison Ashley, adapted for the stage by Richard Tulloch. *The Play Hating Allison Ashley,* Puffin Books, 1988.

Halfway Across the Galaxy and Turn Left, produced as a television series by Crawford Productions, 1992.

Boss of the Pool, adapted for the stage by Mary Morris.

Further Information About the Author
Don't Tell Lucy, Illustrated by Kristen Hilliard, Methuen, 1987.

How Writers Write, Pamela Lloyd, Methuen, 1987.

The Inside Story—Creating Children's Books, editor, Belle Alderman, Children's Book Council of Australia, A.C.T. Branch, 1987.

Coming Out From Under—Contemporary Australian Women Writers, Pam Gilbert, Pandora Press, 1988.

The Story Makers, editor Margaret Dunkle, Oxford University Press, 1987.

MARGARET MAHY
Writings
Juvenile fiction for various ages
A *Lion in the Meadow.* Illustrated by Jenny Williams, Dent, London; Watts, New York, 1969.

The Witch in the Cherry Tree. Illustrated by Jenny Williams, Dent, London; Parents Magazine Press, New York, 1974.

The Bus Under the Leaves. Illustrated by Margery Gill, Dent, London, 1975.

The Boy Who Was Followed Home. Illustrated by Steven Kellogg, Watts, New York, 1975; Dent, London.

The Great Piratical Rumbustification and The Librarian and the Robbers. Illustrated by Quentin Blake, Dent, London, 1978.

The Haunting. Dent, London; Atheneum, New York, 1982.

The Changeover. Atheneum, New York, 1984.

The Catalogue of the Universe. Atheneum, New York, 1985.

Jam: A True Story. Atlantic Monthly Press, Boston, 1985.

The Tricksters. Macmillan, New York, 1986.

The Blood and Thunder Adventures on Hurricane Peak. M. K. McElderry, New York, 1989.

The Great White Man Eating Shark. Illustrated by Jonathan Allen, Dial Books for Young Readers, New York, 1990.

Making Friends. Illustrated by Wendy Smith, M. K. McElderry, New York, 1990.

The Pumpkin Man and the Crafty Creeper. Illustrated by Helen Craig, Lothrop, Lee and Shepard Books, New York, 1990.

The Seven Chinese Brothers. retold traditional story Illustrated by Jean and Mou-Sien Tseng, Scholastic, New York, 1990.

Dangerous Spaces. Viking, New York, 1991.

Keeping House. Illustrated by Wendy Smith, M. K. McElderry, New York, 1991.

Memory. M. K. McElderry, New York, 1991.

Underrunners. Viking, New York, 1992.

A Busy Day for a Good Grandmother. Illustrated by Margaret Chamberlain, M. K. McElderry, New York, 1993.

A Fortunate Name. Illustrated by Marion Young, Delacorte, New York, 1993.

The Good Fortune Gang. Illustrated by Marion Young, Delacorte, New York, 1993.

The Three-Legged Cat. Illustrated by Jonathan Allen, Viking, New York, 1993.

Special Recognition
Awards and honors

Esther Glen Medal, *A Lion in the Meadow,* 1970.

Esther Glen Medal, *The First Margaret Mahy Story Book,* 1972.

Carnegie Medal, *The Haunting,* 1982.

Esther Glen Medal, *The Haunting,* 1983.

Carnegie Medal, *The Changeover,* 1984.

Canty University writer in residence, 1984.

Esther Glen Medal, *The Changeover,* 1985.

New Zealand Lit Fund Award for Achievement, 1985.

AIM Junior Book Award, *Underrunners,* 1993.

Honorary Doctor of Letters, Canterbury University, New Zealand, 1993.

Order of New Zealand, 1993.

JOHN MARSDEN
Writings
Juvenile fiction for various ages
The Journey. Pan Australia, Sydney, 1988.

So Much to Tell You. Walter McVitty Books, Sydney, 1988; Little, Brown, Boston; Fawcett Juniper, New York.

The Great Gatenby. Pan Australia, Sydney, 1989.

Staying Alive in Year 5. Pan Australia, Sydney, 1990.

Letters from the Inside. Pan Australia, Sydney, 1991.

Take My Word for It. Pan Australia, Sydney, 1992.

Looking for Trouble. Pan Macmillan, Sydney, 1993.

Out of Time. Pan Macmillan, Sydney, 1993.

Tomorrow When the War Began. Pan Macmillan, Sydney, 1993.

Nonfiction for young people and adults
> *Everything I Know About Writing.* Mandarin, Port Melbourne, 1993.

Special Recognition
Awards and honors
> Children's Book Council of Australia Book of the Year Award for Older Readers, *So Much to Tell You,* 1988.
>
> Premier's Award Victoria, *So Much to Tell You,* 1988.
>
> Young Adult Book Award New South Wales, *So Much to Tell You,* 1988.
>
> American Library Association Notable Book, *So Much to Tell You,* 1989.
>
> Christopher Medal, *So Much to Tell You,* 1989.
>
> Children's Book Council of Australia Book of the Year Award for Older Readers, *Take My Word For It,* 1993.

IVAN SOUTHALL
Writings
Juvenile fiction for various ages
> *Meet Simon Black.* Angus & Robertson, Sydney, 1950.
>
> *Simon Black in Peril.* Angus & Robertson, Sydney, 1951.
>
> *Simon Black in Space.* Angus & Robertson, Sydney, 1952; Anglobooks, New York, 1953.
>
> *Simon Black in Coastal Command.* Angus & Robertson, Sydney; Anglobooks, New York, 1953.

Simon Black in China. Angus & Robertson, Sydney, 1954.

Simon Black and the Spacemen. Angus & Robertson, Sydney, 1955.

Simon Black in the Antarctic. Angus & Robertson, Sydney, 1956.

Simon Black Takes Over: The Strange Tale of Operation Greenleaf. Angus & Robertson, Sydney, 1959.

Simon Black at Sea: The Fateful Voyage of A.P.M.I. Arion. Angus & Robertson, Sydney, 1961.

Hills End. Illustrated by Jim Phillips, Angus & Robertson, Sydney, 1962; St. Martin's, New York, 1963.

Ash Road. Illustrated by Clem Seale, Angus & Robertson, Sydney, 1965; St. Martin's, New York, 1966.

The Fox Hole. Illustrated by Ian Ribbons, Methuen, London; St. Martin's, New York, 1967.

To the Wild Sky. Illustrated by Jennifer Tuckwell, Angus & Robertson, Sydney; St. Martin's, New York, 1967.

Let the Balloon Go. Illustrated by Ian Ribbons, Methuen, London; St. Martin's, New York, 1968.

Sly Old Wardrobe. picture book Illustrated by Ted Greenwood, F. W. Cheshire, Melbourne, 1968; St. Martin's, New York, 1970.

Finn's Folly. Angus & Robertson, Sydney; St. Martin's, New York, 1969.

Chinaman's Reef Is Ours. Angus & Robertson, Sydney; St. Martin's, New York, 1970.

Bread and Honey. Angus & Robertson, Sydney, 1970; published as *Walk a Mile and Get Nowhere,* Bradbury, Englewood Cliffs, New Jersey, 1970.

Josh. Angus & Robertson, Sydney, 1971; Macmillan, New York, 1972.

Head in the Clouds. Illustrated by Richard Kennedy, Angus & Robertson, London, 1972; Macmillan, New York, 1973.

Over the Top. Illustrated by Ian Ribbons, Methuen, London, 1972; published as *Benson Boy,* Illustrated by Ingrid Fetz, Macmillan, New York, 1973.

Matt and Jo. Angus & Robertson, London; Macmillan, New York, 1973.

Three Novels (includes *The Fox Hole, Let the Balloon Go,* and *Over the Top.* Methuen, London, 1975.

What About Tomorrow. Angus & Robertson, London; Macmillan, New York, 1977.

King of the Sticks. Collins, Sydney, 1979; Methuen, London; Greenwillow, New York, 1979.

The Golden Goose. Methuen, London, Greenwillow, New York; 1981.

The Long Night Watch. Methuen, London, 1983; Farrar, Straus, New York, 1984.

A City Out of Sight. Angus & Robertson, Sydney, 1984; Irwin, Toronto, 1985.

Christmas in the Tree. Hodder & Stoughton, Sydney, 1985.

Rachel. Angus & Robertson, Sydney; Farrar, Straus, New York, 1986.

Blackbird. Farrar, Straus & Giroux, New York, 1988; Mammoth Australia, Port Melbourne, 1992.

The Mysterious World of Marcus Leadbeater. Farrar, Straus & Giroux, New York, 1990; Mammoth Australia, Port Melbourne, 1991.

Juvenile nonfiction
Journey into Mystery: A Story of the Explorers Burke and Wills. Illustrated by Robin Goodall, Lansdowne, Melbourne, 1961.

Lawrence Hargrave. Biography, Oxford University Press, Melbourne, 1964.

Rockets in the Desert. The Story of Woomera. Angus & Robertson, Sydney, 1964.

Indonesian Journey. Lansdowne, Melbourne, 1965; Ginn, Boston; Newnes, London, 1966.

The Sword of Esau: Bible Stories Retold. Illustrated by Joan Kiddell-Monroe, Angus & Robertson, Sydney, 1967; St. Martin's, New York, 1968.

Bushfire! Illustrated by Julie Mattox, Angus & Robertson, Sydney, 1968.

The Curse of Cain: Bible Stories Retold. Illustrated by Joan Kiddell-Monroe, Angus & Robertson, Sydney, 1968; St. Martin's, New York, 1968.

Seventeen Seconds, adaptation of *Softly Tread the Brave.* Hodder & Stoughton, Sydney, 1973; Macmillan, New York, 1973; Brockhampton Press, Leicester, England, 1974.

Fly West. Angus & Robertson, London, 1974; Macmillan, New York, 1975.

Adult fiction

Out of the Dawn: Three Short Stories. privately printed, 1942.

Flight to Gibraltar. Horwitz, Sydney, 1959.

Mediterranean Black. Horwitz, Sydney, 1959.

Sortie in Cyrenaica. Horwitz, Sydney, 1959.

Third Pilot. Horwitz, Sydney, 1959.

Mission to Greece. Horwitz, Sydney, 1960.

Atlantic Pursuit. Horwitz, Sydney, 1960.

Adult nonfiction

The Weaver from Meltham. Whitcombe & Tombs, Melbourne, 1950.

The Story of the Hermitage: The First Fifty Years of the Geelong Church of England Girls' Grammar School. F. W. Chesire, Melbourne, 1956.

They Shall Not Pass Unseen. Angus & Robertson, Sydney, 1956.

A Tale of Box Hill: Day of the Forest. Box Hill City Council, Australia, 1957.

Bluey Truscott: Squadron Leader Keith William Truscott, R.A.A.F., D.F.C. and Bar. Angus & Robertson, Sydney, 1958.

Softly Tread the Brave: A Triumph over Terror, Devilry, and Death by Mine Disposal Officers John Stuart Mouldt and Hugh Randal Syme. Angus & Robertson, Sydney, 1960.

Parson on the Track: Bush Brothers in the Australian Outback. Lansdowne, Melbourne, 1962; Angus & Robertson, London, 1963.

Woomera. Angus & Robertson, Sydney, 1962.

Indonesia Face to Face. Lansdowne, Melbourne, 1964; Angus & Robertson, London, 1965.

The Challenge: Is the Church Obsolete? An Australian Response to the Challenge of Modern Society. Ivan Southall, editor, Lansdowne, Melbourne, 1966.

"Sources and Responses." Lecture, Library of Congress, Washington, D.C., 1973.

"Real Adventure Belongs to Us." May Hill Arbuthnot honor lecture, American Library Association, Chicago, 1974.

A Journey of Discovery: On Writing for Children. Kestrel, London, 1975; Macmillan, New York, 1976.

Scripts and screenplays
Let the Balloon Go. Film Australia, 1975.

RESOURCES AND ADDRESSES

Listed here are addresses for Book Adventures, Inc., Dromkeen, and the libraries mentioned in the text, as well as some bookstores. Since books not published in the United States are not readily available here, I've included information on ordering books by mail from Australia and New Zealand.

Book Adventures
Dr. Mary Lou White
1402 Glen View Rd.
Yellow Springs, Ohio 45387

Dromkeen
Kay Keck, General Manager
Riddell's Creek
Victoria 3431
Australia

Library of New South Wales (Mitchell Library)
Joy Storie, Education Office
Macquarie St.
Sydney 2000
Australia

National Library of New Zealand
For information service—reference and interloan services
P.O. Box 3342
Wellington
New Zealand

BOOK STORES
Dorothy Butler Bookshop
Corner of Jervois and St. Mary's Rds.
Ponsonby, Auckland
New Zealand

Glen Rees says the Dorothy Butler Bookshop specializes in New Zealand children's authors, carrying every one available for readers from birth to 18 years of age. The shop also specializes in books that help parents understand reading requirements of their children and to help foster their children's reading development. They have access to most Australian publishers and hold stocks of Allen & Unwin and Jacaranda Wiley in Auckland. U.S. credit cards: MasterCard, Visa, Diners Club and AMEX are accepted.

Jabberwocky Bookstore
718 Dominion Rd.
Auckland
New Zealand

Jo Noble of Jabberwocky Bookstore says they stock every New Zealand children's book they can find shelf room for, as well as children's books from Australia and the United Kingdom. They supply Australian books from publishers Angus and Robertson, Allen and Unwin, Jacaranda, and D.B. They accept credit card orders from the United States.

The Little Bookroom Pty. Limited
Arthur Ullin
185 Elizabeth Street
Melbourne, Victoria 3000
Australia

Arthur Ullin, managing director, of The Little Bookroom, says that they currently supply credit card orders to a number of teachers and librarians in the United States. MasterCard and Visa are their preferred choices, but they also accept AMEX and Diners Club, although those two take a higher commission.

Incidentally, Mr. Ullin discovered John Marsden's *So Much to Tell You* and, with the help and advice of some friends, who had just started a small publishing company, this book was published.

The Children's Bookshop Pty. Ltd.
Robin Morrow
ACN 002 362 495
12 Hannah Street
Beecroft, New South Wales 2119
Australia

We met Robin Morrow of the Children's Bookshop at the Rozelle Writers' Center near Sydney where she set up a special Story Tour Bookshop so we could buy books by authors we would meet. The Children's Bookshop accepts Bankcard, MasterCard and Visa.

James Bennett Library Services
4 Collaroy Street
Collaroy, New South Wales 2097
Australia

James Bennett Library Services accepts credit card mail orders for both Australian and New Zealand publications.

ABOUT THE AUTHOR

Janet Crane Barley earned a Bachelor of Science in Journalism degree from Bowling Green State University (Ohio) in 1956, when that was a nontraditional choice for women. After graduation she became women's editor of *The Xenia Daily Gazette* (Ohio), then served a stint as an information services officer in the United States Air Force. She joined the Air Force to grow beyond the niche of writing "women's" news and because she wanted to see the world. Later, as a free-lance writer, she sold more than 200 profiles of first-line supervisors in utilities, construction, and manufacturing to the Bureau of Business Practice, a division of Prentice Hall. She loved reading children's books to her daughter, Sandra, and son, Dean, when they were very young and continued to read children's books for herself even after they were grown. She has worked in various public relations-marketing positions, most recently for Hospice of Dayton (Ohio) in its Wilmington and Middletown branches.

DATE DUE

PRINTED IN U.S.A.